# MORALITY FOR MUGGLES

## ETHICS IN THE BIBLE AND THE WORLD OF HARRY POTTER

**Moshe Rosenberg**

KTAV Publishing House, Inc.
Jersey City, New Jersey

Library of Congress Cataloging-in-Publication Data

Rosenberg, Moshe.
  Morality for Muggles : ethics in the Bible and the world of Harry Potter / by Moshe
Rosenberg.
     p. cm.
  Includes bibliographical references (p.      ).
  ISBN 978-1-60280-183-7
  1. Rowling, J. K.--Criticism and interpretation--Juvenile literature. 2. Rowling,
J. K.--Characters--Harry Potter--Juvenile literature. 3. Potter, Harry (Fictitious
character)--Juvenile literature. 4. Ethics in literature--Juvenile literature. 5. Conduct
of life in literature--Juvenile literature. 6. Bible and literature--Juvenile literature.
7. Jewish ethics--Juvenile literature. 8. Conduct of life--Juvenile literature. I. Title.
  PR6068.O93Z849 2011
  823'.914--dc22

                                                              2011028166

Published by
KTAV Publishing House, Inc.
888 Newark Avenue, Suite 119
Jersey City, NJ  07306
Email:  bernie@ktav.com
www.ktav.com
(201) 963-9524
Fax (201) 963-0102

# CONTENTS

# ACKNOWLEDGMENTS

It is a responsibility, but also a pleasure, to remember the many people whose encouragement helped turn whimsical hobby into a dream realized.

Back in 2000, Penny Joel, my assistant teacher, suggested that I read one of the *Harry Potter* books that were so popular with our students. Thank you for starting me on this journey.

Few schools would allow a religious studies teacher to take busloads of kids to see a fantasy movie on school time, and then spend the evening in wizarding activities on school premises. The SAR Academy in Riverdale, New York is such a school. Under the leadership of Rabbi Joel Cohn, and then Rabbi Binyamin Krauss, SAR fosters creativity in and out of the classroom, and is willing to take chances for education. I am privileged to work there.

The enthusiasm of more than a decade of students and their parents, who joyously and chaotically staged Harry Potter Nights with me, energized me to produce this book. You will meet some of those students in these pages.

Members of Congregation Etz Chaim of Kew Gardens Hills, New York, showed remarkable equanimity as their rabbi graduated from being "the Star Trek Rabbi" to being "the Harry Potter Rabbi." Their attitude of acceptance and welcome for all walks of life now even encompasses those of the wizarding world. The congregation's children, fierce and knowledgeable Harry Potter fans, gave me ever more incentive to pursue this project.

Gary Rosenblatt, Publisher of New York's *Jewish Week* had the courage to run my op-ed article on Harry Potter and Judaism that morphed into this book. I am grateful for the professional generosity.

The discerning eye of Bernie Scharfstein of KTAV, who knew there was a book in me before I did, is matched only by his gentleman's manner in shepherding this project to fruition. It is a privilege to work with you and Adam Bengal.

Diana Drew's painstaking copy-editing yielded a much smoother manuscript and Janice Weiss's beautiful layout managed to perfectly capture the character of its contents. Hyla Bolsta for the cover design. Thanks to all of you.

Perhaps the most pleasurable part of the whole process is the support I have received from my family. My brother Mordechai's creative ventures have inspired me to reach high. My brother Abe has long been the source of down-to-earth advice on writing and on life. My children, Yair (who prepared the glossary), Sarah Meira, Gavriel, Hudy, Bracha, Duly, and Yisrael Dovid have been the biggest fans of this book all along, and have caught some of my worst errors before they were enshrined in print. Yair and Sarah Meira, both published authors themselves, generously gave of their skills to polish this manuscript. Few authors are blessed with such talent in their home.

I have often wondered whether I would escape the trap of cliché if I had the chance to dedicate a book to my wife. Dina is the DNA of anything worthwhile in my life. She has the magical ability to overlook my many faults and the enchanting quality of staying in love all these years. May this small book justify some of your many sacrifices and help our children and others reinforce what we try to teach them.

# INTRODUCTION

If I had a knut for every time someone asked me whether the *Harry Potter* novels clash with the Bible's ban on witchcraft, all the vaults of Gringott's wouldn't be able to hold my fortune. Undoubtedly, much could be written on both sides of that issue. But that's not why I wrote this book. Frankly, the question has never bothered me.

But I love Bible. Its study and observance suffuse my life. Its rhythms and poetry are the beat to which I live. As a rabbi, teaching Bible and ethics is what I do.

And I love *Harry Potter.* Not exactly religiously, but it fires my imagination. It resonates within me as only truth does. J. K. Rowling hits so many right notes in describing people, relationships, good and evil.

So this book is an attempt to introduce two of my loves to each other. In it I hope to trace some of life's eternal questions from the vantage point of both Bible and the world of Harry Potter. Issues like love and friendship, parents and children, life and death, good and evil. Sorry, not witchcraft and magic wands.

What will you, the reader, gain from these pages? I hope that you will share some aha! moments, when it becomes clear that what felt so right when it came out of Dumbledore's mouth was also a teaching in *Ethics of the Fathers,* or a *Midrash*, or a Hasidic story. There will be times that an insight from the wizarding world will illuminate a biblical theme or vice versa. Sometimes it will become clear that the two worlds diverge on a particular point or assumption. Most of all, this text will be a welcome pre-text to think about universal themes that give life meaning, and which find expression in holy and secular scripture.

In my life, the nexus of Bible and *Harry Potter* has had a very special application in the world of religious education. But so much of what follows in these pages is of universal value for anyone to whom ethics and life's enduring questions speak.

Every time I open a volume of Harry Potter, I am struck with another topic that should have appeared in this book, or an aspect of one of the chapters that I failed to mention. I am comforted by the fact that God, Himself, left some of His creation unfinished, as well. He by design, and I, by neglect, leave the perfecting of our worlds in your hands.

Here's hoping your reading experience is as magical as the writing process was for me.

### A Note to the Reader

To make the text accessible to readers of widely disparate backgrounds, I have mercilessly excised Hebrew terms, translating them instead. The few that remain are translated and defined in the glossary. Likewise, I have omitted the names of many of the sources cited, inserting instead phrases like "A great Rabbi once explained."This is not, heaven forbid, to deny others the credit they richly deserve, but to make the text flow smoothly, even for those not familiar with the original sources. The missing names can be found in the endnotes to this volume, and if you seek more detailed information, feel free to e-mail me at mosherosenberg1@gmail.com.

It goes without saying that a book about *Harry Potter* is no substitute for reading the actual novels, an activity whose pleasurable rewards I recommend to all!

For the sake of brevity, I have referred to the novels by number of volume, rather than by title or abbreviation. The complete list follows:

*Harry Potter and the Sorcerer's Stone* – Book 1
*Harry Potter and the Chamber of Secrets* – Book 2
*Harry Potter and the Prisoner of Azkaban* – Book 3
*Harry Potter and the Goblet of Fire* – Book 4
*Harry Potter and the Order of the Phoenix* – Book 5
*Harry Potter and the Half-Blood Prince* – Book 6
*Harry Potter and the Deathly Hallows* – Book 7

I have subdivided this book into sections on The Individual, Relationships, Society, and What Matters Most, with each section encompassing several chapters. Between these sections and the notes and glossary, I have included a selection of the writing of my students over the years.

# The Individual

≹

Breaking the Rules

Jealousy

Manners

Repentance

Grief

# BREAKING THE RULES

I could never have been Harry Potter. I was always a good kid who followed the rules. If an adult told me to stay put—I stayed put. If there was a curfew, I was in bed. Truth be told, I was pretty timid, bordering on the wimpy, and if I saw someone breaking the rules, I probably looked appropriately horrified. Sort of like Hermione, when she said, "You could get us killed, or worse—expelled!"

But Harry would not have been Harry if he'd followed rules. He would never have taken those nighttime jaunts under the invisibility cloak, never have gone to the restricted section of the library, never have discovered the Mirror of Erised or the Chamber of Secrets or . . . well, you get the point. The rule breaking that so infuriated Professor Snape is one of the traits that endears Harry to us, the readers. It was what endeared him to Sirius Black, because it was one of James Potter's trademarks, as well. Perhaps we admire Harry for the audacity to do what we would never dare. Perhaps through him we live life on the reckless side.

Even at his rule-flouting worst, Harry doesn't alienate us, because it is clear that he breaks rules out of loyalty and altruism, not just out of mischief. When he ventures into places officially off-limits, he is doing so to protect Hagrid and save Norbert the dragon, to protect the school from the marauding basilisk, to save the wrongly accused Sirius, and so on.

Perhaps most fascinating is that even as Harry's penchant for breaking rules eventually softens up Hermione's "goody good" approach, he discovers that he is not the risk-taker that his father was. Hermione joins Harry and Ron on their illegal escapades, and eventually stoops to the level of confounding Cormac McLaggen. She does so out of loyalty to Ron, who wants to become Quidditch keeper, a motivation she may well have picked up from Harry. Harry, on the other hand, finds himself warning Sirius in Book 5 not to risk a visit to Hogwarts, even in his animal form, and hears Sirius resentfully say, "You're not as much like James as I thought. The risk is what would have made it fun for him." James Potter and, for that matter, Fred and George Weasley, felt that rules were made to be broken and broke rules for the thrill of it. Harry came to realize that his rule breaking was much more limited and purposeful.

Surely rule breaking could not be considered praiseworthy in any religion. Good deeds or commandments are our rules, and it is hard to imagine anyone being viewed in a positive light for violating a commandment.

And yet that is exactly what we find in several different contexts.

Few institutions in Judaism are holier than the *Shabbat*, or Sabbath day, with its thirty-nine forbidden categories of creative activity. And yet we know that when the preservation of life is at stake, we are required to break the rules of the Sabbath to save a life. The preservation of life pushes aside, or supersedes, the Shabbat. In a similar vein, we are taught that when a positive commandment can only be performed through the violation of a prohibition, one is permitted to do the normally forbidden act. Thus a priest, in ancient Israelite times, could wear the required belt for service in the Holy Temple in Jerusalem, even though it contained an otherwise forbidden mixture of wool and linen. The positive commandment supersedes the negative one. These cases are hardly extraordinary. In any legal system, conflicts in values and priorities must be resolved. The system chooses one value over another and, in complying, the individual is not breaking a rule, but observing the overarching rule that determines that one value is more important than another.

A more striking situation would be how the Rabbis forbade the sounding of the *shofar* on the Jewish New Year of Rosh Hashana, the reading of the Scroll of Esther on the holiday of Purim, and the waving of the *lulav* on the holiday of Tabernacles (Sukkot), when these holidays coincide with the Sabbath, in order to ensure that people did not violate the Sabbath in their performance. Yet even here the Rabbis did not order people to actively commit a sin, merely to refrain from performing a commandment.

It really gets interesting when we read in II Kings 19 of Elijah the prophet staging a showdown against the prophets of Ba'al on Mount Carmel. The contest, which involved seeing which God would accept his priests' sacrifice, constituted a direct violation of the biblical prohibition against sacrificing outside of the Temple. Here, on a one-time basis, the prophet permitted an out-and-out sin for the sake of a much greater spiritual gain—proving the superiority of the Hebrew God. Similarly, the Talmud labels the Nazirite a sinner for denying himself the pleasure of wine permitted by the Torah, and yet allows the practice of self-denial to continue. It appears that the "small" sin is being allowed for the sake of a much larger spiritual gain. The Talmud calls this type of rare case a "sin for the sake of heaven," and declares: "A sin for the sake of heaven is as great as a commandment performed not for the sake of heaven." Probably the most famous example of a sin for the sake of heaven is Esther going willingly to King Ahasuerosh in order to save her people.[1]

What is the upshot of all this? Rules can never cover every single situation. There will always be the exceptional case in which adherence to a rule, while praiseworthy, may force a person to pass up the opportunity for immense spiritual gain. Both the Bible and the moral universe of *Harry Potter* allow an honest individual to do a cost/benefit analysis and opt for the small sin. Of course, this is not done lightly, and is permitted exceedingly rarely. The transgressor accepts the consequences of his sin, and the obligation to atone for it. But in the final analysis, as Harry and Esther show us, breaking a rule can lead to the salvation of the entire wizarding world and the entire Jewish people.

# JEALOUSY

One of the climactic moments in Book 7 occurs when Ron has his chance to destroy a horcrux. After dramatically helping Harry recover the sword of Gryffindor, Ron is challenged by Harry to destroy the Slytherin locket that housed a fragment of Voldemort's soul. But when he attempts to do so, the sinister presence inside the locket begins to prey on his deepest fears and insecurities. Taking the form of Harry and Hermione, it taunts him: "What have you ever done, compared with the Chosen One? What are you, compared with the Boy Who Lived?" These words reawaken in Ron the feelings we had glimpsed before when he berated Harry for entering the Tri-Wizard Tournament in Book 4. Ron, ever the loyal sidekick, who seems to have no ego at all, is reminded that he plays nothing more than second fiddle to the great Harry Potter. Part of him has always wondered what gifts he can possibly bring to the table, both at home, where every niche of space seems to have been claimed by siblings, and in his relationship with Harry and Hermione, where they provide the courage and the brains. Part of Ron's charm is that he cannot see his own strengths, but that trait is targeted by the horcrux as it tries to fan his insecurity into full-fledged jealousy.

In the end, Ron sees through the ploy and destroys the locket. He overcomes the latent jealousy that threatened to engulf him. He chooses the words of the real Harry and the real Hermione over those of the horcrux version, which mimicked his own dreaded forebodings. He makes peace with his role in the triad of young wizards who would save the wizarding world. And, in the end, it is he who gets the girl, not Harry. Ron even reaches the point where he can joke about his supporting-role status. In the epilogue, when he takes his children to platform 9 3/4 and many children on the Hogwarts Express turn to stare at Harry, Ron tells little Albus, "It's me. I'm extremely famous."

The closest biblical parallel to Ron's banishing of jealousy is found in the complicated relationship of Moses and Aaron. Aaron, who as firstborn had every reason to expect to be chosen as the leader and prophet, accepts the role of interpreter and second-in-command. Is he happy about it? When God reunites the brothers as their mission begins, He tells Moses that Aaron will be sincerely glad for him. "He will see you and be glad in his heart" (Ex. 4:14). The Midrash comments that the purity of Aaron's heart earned him the right to wear the High Priest's apron over his heart. While a reward for letting Moses lead, this is also a way of giving Aaron his chance to shine as a leader in his own right.

But this idyllic state of affairs does not go undisturbed. In the wilderness, after bouts of complaints that climax in the sin of the spies, even Moses's two siblings turn against him and murmur: "Did God only speak with him? Surely He spoke with us as well" (Num. 12:2). Their dissatisfaction earns Miriam a punishment of leprosy and induces Aaron to plead for her recovery from Moses. God Himself gives them a lecture about Moses, calling him not "the Chosen One," but "my most faithful servant" (v. 7). (This is a term used by Voldemort's followers in a very different way.) The message is clear: Know your place.

It is curious that in this relationship, the potential jealousy runs both ways. There is a rich Midrashic literature depicting the parts of Aaron's life that Moses envied, starting from the position of high priest, and including his peaceful death and the knowledge that his sons would succeed him. It is as if to say: The people you most envy are busy envying you, so don't waste your energy. Just make the most of your own gifts

An optimistic message about human nature emerges from both stories. Jealousy is part of the human condition and is to be expected. Not all of us can be wholehearted in our joy over other people's good fortune. Even Aaron, who began that way, slipped, and had to be restored to his better self. Perhaps the best depiction of that struggle is how Harry fights with himself to be genuinely happy when Ron is chosen as prefect—and he is not. Harry recognizes the envy in his heart, and doesn't like what he sees. He argues with himself until he feels his smile and words of praise for Ron begin to sound more natural, more sincere.

We are not condemned for our inner thoughts of jealousy, unless we give in to them and act upon them. When the Bible bids us, "Thou shall not covet" (Ex. 20:14), the great medieval Jewish authority Maimonides rules that one only violates the prohibition against coveting something belonging to another if one takes action to obtain it. While we must work at the character trait and uproot jealousy from our souls, this ruling, like the inner dialogue in Harry's mind, reminds us that the struggle is ongoing and that we must not get down on ourselves for simply being human.

# MANNERS

*"Good evening, Amycus," said Dumbledore, calmly, as though welcoming the man to a tea party. "And you've brought Alecto, too... Charming..."*

*The woman gave an angry little titter. "Think your jokes'll help you on your deathbed then?"*

*"Jokes? No, no, these are manners," replied Dumbledore.* (Book 7)

★ ✦ ✦ ✦

*Seven traits distinguish a wise person . . . the wise person does not speak before someone greater in wisdom than he . . . and does not interrupt the speech of another . . . (Ethics of the Fathers 5:6)*

Albus Dumbledore, headmaster of Hogwarts, lies propped up against the stones of the Astronomy tower, his strength ebbing away from drinking the noxious potion in which Lord Voldemort had stored a horcrux. Before help can arrive, Draco Malfoy bursts in and disarms the headmaster. While he wavers in his resolve to murder Dumbledore, the Carrows—brother and sister Death Eaters who had terrorized the school in his absence—break through the chaos of the battle that is raging below and join Draco, only to be greeted by their victim with … manners.

One of the many lessons Albus Dumbledore transmits to his students and readers alike is that there is no such thing as "mere manners." When we are polite, we are not simply observing the conventions of our society. When we are civil, we are not just abiding by some social contract. We are expressing our essence. We are showing who we are.

Whenever Harry, in his resentment, refers to his potions master as "Snape," Dumbledore unfailingly corrects him: "Professor Snape." Just because someone does not behave well toward you does not mean that you may sink to a level of incivility. That would not be true to yourself.

When Dumbledore comes to pick Harry up from the Dursleys in the beginning of Book 6, he is met with a rude reception. His reaction is to supply the manners that the Dursleys were so sorely lacking. He conjures a glass of mead for each of the group. Like the Carrows, the Dursleys don't know what to make of the "manners" of Dumbledore, and refuse to take their glass and drink, even after the glasses repeatedly remind them by tapping them on the head. Dumbledore chides them that it would have been more polite to drink what they were offered. The whole scene is comical, but beneath the humor is the consistent message that manners are not negotiable.

Dumbledore's unfailing courtesy, even when not reciprocated, is echoed in the behavior of Moses and Aaron toward Pharaoh at the beginning of their mission to rescue the Hebrew nation. "God commanded them regarding the children of Israel and regarding Pharaoh, king of Egypt" (Ex. 6:13). The Midrash explains: God commanded them to give Pharaoh the honor due to a king. But wait—about whom are we speaking? This is the monarch who enslaved nations, who murdered babies, and who responded to requests for relief with cruel crackdowns. Is honor due to such a king? Apparently, sometimes we give honor to another because of who *he* is, and sometimes because of who *we* are.

Our manners remind us of our inherent dignity and self-worth, and we never need the reminder more than when others are trying to dehumanize us. Indeed, it is in the darkest moments of Jewish history that our greatest heroes have clung to their identity by holding onto the ordinary routines and protocols and courtesies of more normal times. Here is a sample from the Talmud, which recounts the martyrdom of a great sage:

> On their return, they found Rabbi Hanina b. Teradyon studying the Torah publicly with the Holy Scrolls in his bosom; he was enwrapped in the Holy Scrolls and surrounded with vines, which were kindled. And two woolen towels, soaked in water, were placed on his heart that his soul might not depart so quickly. When his daughter said to him: Alas, Father, that I should see you thus! He answered: If I were burned alone, it would be hard for me, but now that I am burned in conjunction with the Holy Scrolls, I am sure that He who will avenge the Holy Scrolls will avenge me, as well. His disciples questioned him: What do you see now? And he answered: I see parchment burning, but letters flying in the air. They said to him: Rabbi, open your mouth, so that the fire should catch you, and he answered: It is better that my soul be taken by Him who gave it and that I myself not cause it an earlier death.[2]

When Rabbi Hanina ben Teradyon, wrapped in the burning coils of a Torah scroll, converses with his students about the propriety of hastening his own death, the maintaining of the teacher-student bond is a form of "manners" that gives structure and comfort to the bleakest of scenarios. Such scenes of civilized behavior amid savagery are common in the literature surrounding the martyrdom of the Rabbis at the hands of their Roman persecutors.

Taking this idea a step further, it can be argued that keeping one's manners and civility at such a moment is a way of denying victory to an enemy who cannot be defeated in any other way. You may disarm me, confine me, even deprive me of my life, but you cannot take from me who I am.

When one Jew smuggled a prayer book into a concentration camp and passed it around so that others could pray, he denied the Nazi enemy their goal of dehumanizing the Jews. And when another shared a precious ration of bread to keep a fellow inmate alive, the act expressed his true essence and his refusal to be reduced to the level of a beast.

In a final twist, Tamir Granot, a contemporary teacher of the Holocaust, quotes a story in which the Nazis did not merely oppress Jews physically, but tried to deny them their "manners," as well, only to have the tables turned on them:

When the Nazi fiend Globochnik arrived in Lublin at the end of 1939, he ordered the chairman of the *Judenrat*, Dr. Wahrman, to assemble all the Jewish people for a general census, in the field at the outskirts of the city. When a sizable Jewish crowd had gathered, disconcerted and frightened by the club-bearing thugs, he suddenly issued the strange order that all the Jews should dance before him to a joyful and jubilant Hasidic melody. Someone in the midst of the crowd began to sing the heart-rending Hasidic tune "Let Us Reconcile, Our Father in Heaven," but the song did not rouse the terrified crowd. Immediately, Globochnik ordered his thugs to beat the Jews, who were refusing to obey his order. As the Nazis fell upon the Jews with unbridled fury, an anonymous voice burst from the assemblage with power and audacity: "We will outlast them, our Father in heaven!" And instantly the song spread among the entire crowd, who entered into a sizzling and passionate dance before their enemies' eyes. The assembled Jews were swept away by the soulful melody, which was now infused with an additional message of faith and trust: "We will outlast them, our Father in heaven!" The crowd grew so enthusiastic that Globochnik stood in his place, confused and bewildered at the faces of Jews singing their song of eternal faith, and he screamed in his murderous voice, "Stop! Immediately!"

Granot explains how the "normal" protocol for Nazi torment of their Jewish prisoners was here reversed. Whereas the typical arrangement saw the victims give up control of their physical fate in the unspoken understanding that they would be allowed the dignity of their stoic acceptance, here, with his command to dance, the Nazi commandant violated that tacit pact. But instead of yielding to the new terms, the victims, by playing this harrowing "game" all too well, turned the tables on the man who would deny them even their "manners."[3]

No, manners are far from trivial in the life of religious person and wizard alike. They remind us of the part of ourselves that no one can take away.

# REPENTANCE

Human beings are imperfect. Along the road to a moral life, we stumble and fall, giving in to temptation and sin. But Judaism is optimistic about the possibility of picking ourselves up and mending our ways, no matter how many tries it takes. "Seven times shall the righteous man fall, but then rise again" (Prov. 24:16). The process of repair is called *teshuva* (meaning, literally, "return") and the person who returns, or tries to mend his ways, is called a *ba'al teshuva*.

The most famous penitent in the Bible is King David. After demonstrating remarkable self-control and trust in God on his way to the throne, and orchestrating a stunning series of military victories and other accomplishments, David is attracted to Bathsheba, wife of Uriah the Hittite. David finds a way to be with her, and sends her husband to his death on the battlefield. Some biblical scholars, in evaluating these sins, conclude that David was not all that different from the power-hungry despots of other nations. Other commentators stake out the opposite position, accepting the most far-fetched arguments to excuse David's actions. The middle approach, which acknowledges both the sin and David's core morality, portrays David as the ultimate man capable of change—the model for all *ba'alei teshuva* of the future. He is the man "who set an example of repentance."[4]

A curious counterpart to David appears in the world of *Harry Potter*. Professor Severus Snape, after initially following Lord

Voldemort and being a Death Eater, repents of his choice and becomes a spy for the Order of the Phoenix. His true loyalties and the story behind them only become clear toward the end of the final book, when he shares his memories with Harry, shortly before dying of the wounds inflicted by Voldemort's snake, Nagini.

There are some striking parallels between David and Snape. Both are motivated by the love of a woman whose son is the subject of prophecy, and each one later brings peace to his respective universe. Both have reason to despise this child, but protect him and groom him for his future role because of his mother. Both think they can bring about the ideal society, only to realize that it is the child who will have that role. Both leave that child a last will and testament that clarifies matters from the past and makes his future path clearer.

The repentance of both David and Snape shuns sentimentality. After recognizing the error of their ways, they do not live happily ever after. Neither is absolved of his guilt, but merely spared death in order to live in the world that his choice formed, and atone for his sin through constructive living. David must rule Israel, even as his family unravels, and prepare the way for the ascent of Solomon, son of Bathsheba. Snape must protect the son of Lily Potter, whose death he did not prevent, and prepare the way for Harry's ascent as "the Boy Who Lived" and "the Chosen One." Both teach us that repentance does not mean that you are spared the consequences of your errors—only that you get a chance to live a life that proves that sin was merely an aberration, not a natural state.

# GRÎEF

eading *Harry Potter* as grief therapy? Why not?

Three of the most courageous members of my synagogue are a boy and two girls whose parents passed away within a span of four years, leaving them orphaned and living with their uncle and aunt in my community. Fortunately, this uncle and aunt are nothing like the Dursleys, and the children found friends and a new life in their new home. But that's not to say that it has always been easy. One of the things that has made the transition a little more bearable for them is their attachment to *Harry Potter,* which their mother used to read to them every night. At their mother's funeral, I referred to the books when speaking directly to the children. When little else could reach them, this could. When you think about it, it makes a lot of sense.

After all, the entire *Harry Potter* saga can be read as the attempts of a boy, orphaned at the age of one, to overcome the loss of his parents. From early, counterproductive attempts, Harry progresses to more mature and effective strategies, culminating in a reunion in Book 7 which neatly ties up the issue.

Book 1 finds Harry transfixed before the Mirror of Erised, mesmerized by a view of the parents he never knew. Dumbledore warns him that neither truth nor wisdom can be attained by pining away for the inaccessible. (This warning echoes powerfully in Book 7, when Harry finally realizes that Dumbledore would see his own parents and sister in the mirror, and even tried rashly to revive them with the Resurrection Stone.)

One of my sixth-grade students wrote that Harry's seeing the parents he couldn't have is like Moses ascending Mount Nebo, from which he was allowed to gaze at the Promised Land, but not enter it.[5] Both scenes share the longing, the tantalizing feel of something just out of reach.

Book 2 provides Harry with a more conventional, if less dramatic way to recall his parents. At the end of the book, Hagrid gives him an album of photographs featuring them.

Only in Book 3 does J.K. Rowling foreshadow the true solution to Harry's dilemma. Toward the book's close, Harry and Sirius are surrounded by a group of dementors, who are closing in and attempting to perform the "kiss" that will suck the soul from both, leaving them worse than dead. When his last try at producing a Patronus to drive them away fails, Harry looks frantically for help, and sees a figure that looks like his father. As the last of Harry's strength ebbs, he sees a stag-shaped Patronus burst from the figure's wand. It gallops toward him, scatters the dementors, and returns to the wand that cast it. Harry harbors the hope that it was his father who had saved him.

But the story's conclusion proves otherwise. When Harry and Hermione are able to go back several hours in time and change events, Harry realizes that he himself was the figure who had saved them. His remarkable outward resemblance to his father accounts for his mistaken impression that his father had been present. In fact, Harry has taken the place of his father, and his own Patronus, also a stag like his father's, had been the one that defeated the dementors.

The message is clear: We overcome the loss of those whom we love by becoming like them and carrying on their work. Harry becomes his father in this most ingenious way. Now he resembles his father not only in outward appearance, but in his actions, as well.

But the father he ultimately becomes is not the romanticized figure from the Mirror of Erised, nor the heroic image of Quidditch fame, nor even the stereotypical father who bursts from Voldemort's wand at the end of Book 4. In Book 5 Harry learns of his father's imperfections through the visions of the pensieve, and eventually realizes that the man he idealized had undergone a process of development to become the person he was. The same man Lily had called "an arrogant toe rag" could mature and win her heart. Harry's understanding of his father becomes more realistic, and makes it possible for him to become a true father figure, as well, when the time comes.

Harry's development bears many similarities to the life path of the biblical Joseph. When Joseph, deprived of his father, is tempted toward sin by the wife of his master, Potiphar, the Midrash says that the only thing that prevents him from yielding to temptation is seeing the image of his father before his eyes.[6] Some commentators have speculated that Joseph actually looked like his father, and, in fact, saw his own reflection, which evoked the memory of his father. Many Midrashim play up the similarities between Joseph and his father, inside and out.[7] Most striking for our purposes is how Joseph begins as the son, but, after losing his father, assumes the role of father figure to the whole family, saving them from famine and supporting them in Egypt, even as Harry, upon defeating Voldemort, becomes the father figure to all those he rescues. Joseph tells his father that God has "made me a father to Pharaoh" (Gen. 45:8), and that role clearly extends to his own family as well.

Robert Nozick, who served as Professor of Philosophy at Harvard, writes,

> When children are young, it is the task of parents to manage the relationship, to monitor it and keep it continuing on a somewhat even keel. During some brief period, perhaps, that responsibility becomes more equal, and then, before one has had time to notice it, it becomes the now-grown-up child's task to maintain the relationship, sometimes to pamper parents, to humor them, to avoid subjects that upset them, and to comfort the surviving one. If adolescence is sometimes marked by rebelling against one's parents and adulthood by becoming independent of them, what marks maturity is becoming a parent to them.[8]

Joseph becomes his father's father, smoothing the way for Jacob's descent to Egypt, avoiding the subject of his brothers' treachery, making his father's waning years the most pleasant of his life. The seventeen years of Joseph "parenting" his father, writes a medieval biblical commentator,[9] correspond to the seventeen years that Jacob parented him.

Beyond assuming the material responsibilities of a father, Joseph takes on the moral and ethical ones, as well, sometimes continuing the work of Jacob, sometimes even correcting it. Where Jacob's favoritism caused dissension and split the family, Joseph's forgiveness re-forges it. Under Joseph's skillful tutelage, his brothers repent, defending, rather than abandoning

Benjamin, and are able to watch with acceptance, rather than jealousy, as Benjamin receives disproportionate gifts from the viceroy. They have learned that while their father may have erred, their reaction had also been exaggerated and inexcusable.

This is how Joseph comes to occupy a quasi-patriarchal role in the founding of the Jewish people. While the *Talmud* insists that "Only three may be termed Fathers of the nation," Jewish mysticism seems to feel otherwise. When the Talmud insists that the three daily prayers cannot derive from the patriarchs alone, because there is no patriarch to whom to ascribe the additional Sabbath prayer, the mystical work *Zohar* suggests that the additional prayer be attributed to Joseph.

This concept of becoming a parent to one's parent is embedded in the very word *patronus,* derived from the Latin root meaning "father." In the absence of a father, the patronus can act in *loco parentis*, protecting as a father would. But in the dramatic climax of Book 7, when Harry's parents, along with Lupin and Sirius, accompany him to the Forbidden Forest to lay down his life as his parents had, their presence acts like a Patronus, ushering him safely past the dementors along the way. It isn't his parents who are replacing the patronus, but the patronus that had, for a time, represented them. At the moment that Harry's transformation from son to parent is completed through the ultimate act of self-sacrifice, it could be argued that he is his own Patronus, without even casting a Patronus charm. He has finally mastered the responsibilities of mature parenthood.

As Professor Nozick writes, "Being grown-up is a way of no longer being a child, hence a way of relating to one's parents, not just by acting as their parent, but by stopping needing or

expecting them to act as yours; and this includes stopping expecting the world to be a symbolic parent, too."[10] Harry carries
within him the gifts of his parents and of the other role models
of his life, but he embraces his role as the one who must perform
his duties without a parent's approval. He realizes that it is time
for him to ease the maturing process of others, helping them
overcome loss and insecurity, as he has.

# Relationships

⚡

## Friendship

## Parents and Children

## Teachers and Students

# FRIENDSHIP

Literature gave us the *Three Musketeers*. Comedy gave us the *Three Stooges*. Even science fiction supplied Kirk, Spock, and McCoy. Now fantasy has its latest trio: Harry, Ron, and Hermione.

It's not accidental that heroes come in threes. Heroism and accomplishment require a blend of talents almost impossible to find in one individual. It is the merging of three personalities that makes the story possible, and the friendship among three very different natures both causes sparks and sparks our interest.

Looked at this way, the best biblical friendship to compare to that of Harry, Ron, and Hermione is not the classic friendship of David and Jonathan, singled out in *Ethics of the Fathers* 5:16, but that of the siblings who led the Jews out of Egypt: Moses, Aaron, and Miriam.

The members of each group are anything but equal. Harry is front and center, with the others clearly relegated to a supporting role. This role does not always sit well with them. Book 4 finds Harry at odds with Ron, and, to a lesser extent, Hermione, over his sudden fame as a tournament champion. Even more so, in Book 7, Ron actually deserts his companions and sees his jealous nightmares and resentments played out graphically by the horcrux locket. To his credit, he overcomes this appeal to his weaker side and destroys the locket.

The moment of jealousy for Aaron and Miriam occurs in Numbers 12, when the two speak disparagingly about their brother: "Did God speak only to Moses? Surely He spoke to us, as well" (v. 2). Miriam is punished with leprosy and both she and Aaron are lectured by God about the unique status of Moses. To their credit, they absorb the lesson, and harmony restored.

It is more challenging to analyze the delicate chemistry among the members of each trio. We are given a hint about the specific contributions to the triumvirate of Harry and his friends at the end of Book 1. After they penetrate all the defenses protecting the Sorcerer's Stone, and prevent it from falling into the hands of Lord Voldemort, they are awarded house points by Dumbledore. Harry's points are given "for pure nerve and outstanding courage." Hermione's are "for the use of cool logic in the face of fire." In other words, Harry is the heart and Hermione is the brains. Ron, however, is rewarded "for the best-played game of chess Hogwarts has seen in many years." This doesn't seem to capture his role and we need to find more evidence of what he contributes to their friendship. It is only after seeing him stick to Harry through thick and thin, saving goals for Harry's Quidditch team and absorbing a love potion meant for his beloved friend, that we really see his strength. Watching Ron always come back for more, despite all his inner struggles, we finally realize what lies at the heart of his character. He has the stolid decency of Sherlock Holmes's Watson and Samuel Johnson's Boswell, but above all he has their unswerving loyalty. That is the quality that makes him indispensable to the story, and which, ultimately, wins him the affections of Hermione.

Ron's other major contribution to the threesome is the invaluable element of humor. Though you don't award house points for it, without Ron's often unintended humor, Harry and Hermione would come across as two precocious teenagers who take themselves much too seriously. By puncturing their earnestness, and daring to call Dumbledore "mental," Ron speaks for us, the readers, and brings the doings of the group within our reach and scope of experience.

Loyalty is certainly a key underpinning in the relationship between Aaron and Moses. As the older brother and preexisting prophet, Aaron had every right to resent God's choosing his younger brother over him to lead the people, and yet, the Almighty Himself testifies: "He shall see you and rejoice in his heart." Aaron was willing to assume the role of interpreter and subordinate, and, but for one brief lapse, remained the faithful second.

The relative roles of Moses and Aaron are captured by a Midrash that compares the mourning periods following their passing. While Moses's death is lamented by "the children of Israel,"[11] Aaron's is mourned by "the *whole house* of Israel."[12] Moses, the Midrash explains, is the majestic lawgiver, concerned with principle over individual. "Let the law pierce the mountain,"[13] and let the chips fall where they may! Aaron, on the other hand, is "a lover and pursuer of peace, who loved God's creatures and brought them near to Torah."[14] Aaron negotiates peace between spouses and between feuding neighbors, making it unnecessary for Moses to apply the laws of divorce or convene a civil court. Perhaps Aaron is thus continuing his role as Moses's interpreter before Pharaoh, communicating the human face of the law that Moses handed down from God, showing that the law works in life, and not just in theory. But making the law fit the people, rather than vice versa, may come with a steep price. Some blame

Aaron for the sin of the golden calf, arguing that he should not have been so accommodating to the people. And yet it is precisely because of his caring for each person—righteous or sinner—that Aaron is so universally loved, and later mourned.

Miriam's role is more subtle and might be clarified through another Midrash. When Miriam's death is followed, in Numbers 21, by a shortage of water for the Israelites, the Midrash comments that the miraculous well that accompanied the nation through the wilderness was a gift of from God in the merit of Miriam. To connect Miriam to water in the parched desert is to label her as no less than a provider of biological life. In this role, Miriam is repeating the act of ensuring her brother's life, as she waited for him at the waters of the Nile. She is thus likewise identified by many commentators as one of the lifesaving midwives, endangering herself to give life to Jewish baby boys, who otherwise would have faced a watery death.

If we put together all that we have discovered about their lives, we can see that Moses, Aaron, and Miriam, like Harry, Ron, and Hermione, complement each other well. Moses is the Lawgiver and Miriam the Lifegiver, while Aaron bridges the two of them, by showing that Law and Life can coexist.

# Parents and Children

*Joseph still lives!* (Gen. 45:25)

*Is Draco alive?* (Narcissa Malfoy, Book 7)

*Take your son, your only son, the one you love—take Isaac.* (Gen. 22:2)

C an parents be expected to sacrifice their child for a higher cause?

The Bible and *Harry Potter* offer different answers to that question. Or do they?

Both certainly agree on many things.

To begin with, both recognize the power of a parent's love. Lily Potter's love and sacrifice for Harry provide him with enchanted protection from even the Killing Curse. Rachel, in her desperation to have a child, says to Jacob, "Give me children or I am as good as dead."[15] When he fears that Joseph is dead, Jacob says, "I shall go to my grave still mourning my son."[16]

In both worlds, we see parents devotedly attached to children whose endearing qualities are not at all obvious. An Isaac can love an Esau and Eli the priest can love his wicked sons, just as Dudley, Draco, and Percy have doting parents. Parental love, it appears, is blind.

There is even a physical symbol of parental love that both worlds have in common. Molly Weasley's motherly love is expressed through the sweaters she knits for her children and for Harry, her honorary child. At first, Fleur does not rate a sweater, which is the same as saying that she is not welcome in the family. Like Molly, Hannah makes a cloak for her son, Samuel, and brings it to him in Shilo.[17] That cloak comes to be Samuel's trademark, and even when he is conjured from the dead to speak to Saul, he is wearing it.

All is fine until the parent is asked to sacrifice his or her child on the altar of some higher authority.

In the book of Genesis (cp. 22), Abraham, who waited until the age of one hundred to finally have a son with his wife, Sarah, is commanded by God to take that very son and offer him as a sacrifice on Mount Moriah. Abraham complies, making the three-day journey, binding Isaac on the altar, and raising his dagger to strike, before being restrained by an angel from heaven. One message that can be taken from the story is that love of God and obedience to His command must transcend even the love for one's own child.

A very different impression emerges from the *Harry Potter* saga. Lucius and Narcissa Malfoy, who willingly betray the entire wizarding world to follow Lord Voldemort, appear to have no greater loyalty than to the Dark Lord. But that is only until their loyalty to him clashes with their love for their son, Draco. In Book 7, when Lord Voldemort thinks he has finally killed Harry, he sends Narcissa to see if Harry is really dead. Narcissa knows that the only way she will be able to find and rescue her son, who is in Hogwarts, will be to enter the castle with the army of Death Eaters. That will only happen if Voldemort is convinced that Harry is dead. And so, although she knows that Harry is still alive, she pronounces him dead, betraying Voldemort to save her son.

On the flip side, Xenophilius Lovegood, who had shown extraordinary courage in publishing Harry's account of the return of Voldemort, finds his loyalty to truth tested when Death Eaters abduct his daughter, Luna, and will only return her in exchange for Harry. For the love of his daughter, Lovegood betrays Harry and almost delivers him into the hands of Lord Voldemort.

The behavior of the Malfoys and Lovegood is consistent with the recurring theme of the power of love, and particularly parental love, in the *Harry Potter* novels. And Harry, the beneficiary of his mother's love and sacrifice, who is told so often by Dumbledore that his advantage over Voldemort is his ability to love, absorbs the lesson so well that it is the cause of his harshest words to Lupin, his friend and mentor. In Book 7, Lupin reveals to Harry that he has left his wife, Tonks, and their child with her parents. Harry turns on Lupin and berates him mercilessly for deserting his child, while Ron looks on, horrified. Harry, who has seen every father figure he's ever known snatched away by death, knows better than anyone that a father does not desert his child for anything, if he can possibly help it.

Must we conclude that in the world of *Harry Potter* there is no higher loyalty for a parent than to a child, but that, according to the Bible, one's loyalty to God must come first? Hasn't every schoolchild wondered, at least fleetingly, after learning the biblical story of the binding of Isaac: "But what would my parents do if God gave them the command He gave Abraham? Would they choose God over me?"

A Midrash and a comment of a great rabbi may provide a way out. The Midrash connects three phrases of the same verse to the cases of attempted or actual child sacrifice in the Bible: "That which I never commanded" (that is, I never intended for Abraham to slaughter his son); "nor spoke" (to Jephtah to sacrifice his daughter); "nor did it enter my heart—" (referring to Meisha, king of Moab).[18] The abomination of child sacrifice is depicted as the furthest thing from the wishes of a merciful God.

The Rabbi adds that the angel restraining Abraham from going through with Isaac's sacrifice is the ultimate proof that there can never be a conflict between love for one's child and love for one's God. It is God who implants within us the love of our children, so that we can emulate the love that He has for all His creatures. Emanating from the same source, love of God and love of children cannot be at odds.[19]

It is no wonder, then, that one of the most common metaphors used in the Bible and by the Rabbis to express the relationship between God and the Jewish people is that of father and son. The comparison underscores the elemental and unconditional nature of God's love. It is a love that can withstand the vicissitudes of history and the folly of faithlessness. To forsake His people would mean that God would condemn Himself eternally to the bereft state of Jacob. It would be to flout the rules of nature He Himself designed. It is as if God's love for us is His own Unbreakable Vow.

# TEACHERS AND STUDENTS

Anyone who was ever a student can recount stories of teachers who changed the course of his or her life for the better—or for the worse. After parents, and sometimes even transcending parents, teachers are the major adult influence in our lives as we grow and develop, and far beyond our school years. It is not surprising that the worlds of Hogwarts and Torah have much to say on the teacher-student relationship.

In justifying the obligation to return a teacher's lost item before that of a parent, the Talmud explains that while a parent brings a child into this world, a spiritual guide brings him into the World to Come.[20] In other words, a child's genetic universe is a gift of his parents, but it is his teachers who design his spiritual landscape. The way I approach adversity, interact with others, order my values, and set my goals, is often the product of the teachers who inspired me. They may exert that influence intentionally or without even realizing it. The student may consciously absorb that influence or only realize its effect down the line.

A contemporary rabbi described the impact made upon his development by his late teacher, saying: "Thank you, my revered teacher. Thank you for fashioning my spiritual world, for the legitimization that you gave me to be myself, for calming me down at difficult moments, for teaching me not to become alarmed by human weaknesses."[21]

It seems that imparting knowledge is the least of the teacher's tasks.

Of all the professors Harry has at Hogwarts, Remus Lupin best fits the bill as a *rebbe*, or mentor, in this sense. As a contemporary and friend of Harry's parents, he is predisposed to take an interest not only in Harry's academic progress, but in his inner life and struggles as well. As a werewolf, Lupin also understands what it means to feel like an outsider in one's own community and to have to struggle just to get by. Though he intercedes many times on Harry's behalf, the most striking interaction comes when he teaches Harry the Patronus Charm.

In Book 3, Harry finds that he has an uncharacteristically severe reaction to the presence of dementors. While these malevolent creatures drive out joy and optimism from all humans by causing them to relive their darkest moments, and are thus the perfect guards for the wizarding prison of Azkaban, Harry's friends have few such memories to fear. Harry, on the other hand, finds himself re-experiencing the night when Voldemort murdered his parents and tried to kill him. It is his mother's screams that echo in his mind and send him into a swoon. When his Slytherin antagonists use this weakness against him, Harry feels only shame. It is here that Professor Lupin changes Harry's life forever.

To begin with, the Patronus Charm Lupin teaches Harry is normally reserved for much older students. When Lupin agrees to teach it to Harry, his decision reflects an educational philosophy grounded in the belief of teaching students based on their particular stage of development, rather than their age. It is also a statement of trust in Harry's ability, which could only inspire self-confidence in the young wizard. But it is the substance of the charm that is truly magical in any universe. In the face of circumstances that are draining all positive feeling from the practitioner, the Patronus Charm requires its practitioner to envision something—anything—joyful in his life, and then, having created a sense of happiness where none existed before, to unleash its image to chase away the specters of negativity.

What more powerful life lesson can a teacher impart? What teacher has not sought, at one time or another, to communicate the idea that joy is to be experienced despite the events of life—not because of them—and that we are in control of that experience? How many Jewish images does this lesson conjure up—tales of Jews in the most adverse conditions, who refused to allow the *simcha* to be drained from their lives and their holidays? I well remember standing before my congregation at times of trial and declaring that, for a Jew, happiness is something we create, not merely a reaction to inspiring events.

The surest evidence that the lesson was not lost on Harry is the fact that he passes it on. When he forms the DA, an underground student fighting force, he teaches his friends how to conjure their own Patronus. And, as most fortunate teachers discover, there comes a time when he is surpassed in this skill by his own students. As the Battle of Hogwarts is raging in Book 7, Harry finds himself, Ron, and Hermione unable to maintain their own Patronuses in the presence of a swarm of dementors, when Luna, Ernie, and Seamus successfully cast theirs. It is Luna, whose mother died tragically and whose idiosyncrasies have made her the butt of jokes, who encourages Harry, saying, "Come on . . . think of something happy . . . We're all still here . . . we're still fighting."

That moment echoes the lesson of an exquisite Hasidic story. The story recounts how the starving and beleaguered Jews of the concentration camp gathered to light a makeshift menorah on the first night of Hanukkah. The Hasidic rabbi presiding over the gathering made the three blessings, but paused before reciting the third. When he was asked later by a secular Jew how he could praise God for "keeping us alive and allowing us to reach this day," he responded that the same question had crossed his mind, and made him pause. But as he surveyed the assembled Jews, and saw how, despite all that had befallen them and all that was likely to come, they had still mustered the courage to light their lone feeble candle, he concluded that this alone was cause enough for the blessing of thanks.[22]

Yet, as we know from experience, not all teachers are positive role models. Like anyone wielding power over others, a teacher may betray that trust and abuse his charges. One need only glance at the newspapers to find instances of clergy and teacher abuse that bear this out. J.K. Rowling supplies us with two examples of such teachers: Severus Snape, who abuses his students emotionally, and Dolores Umbridge, who abuses them physically, as well.

As we learn the truth about Snape's past, we better understand his treatment of Harry, although we do not excuse it. At its best, Snape's behavior is blatant favoritism toward his House, but often it is the belittling of the character and abilities of students who have displeased him, especially Harry. Sometimes it seems as if he is simply inclined to interpret anything Harry does in the most negative light possible. (This is exactly the behavior of King Saul toward David, once his paranoia sets it.) But other times the insults are gratuitous, the punishments disproportionate, and the language inexcusably demeaning.

From Snape we learn what can happen if a teacher brings his own baggage into the classroom. Snape's unrequited love of Lily Potter and his disdain for James Potter have no place in his potions dungeon. When a teacher cannot check his prejudices at the door, it is time to take a leave of absence.

But Snape's sniping pales in comparison to the cold-blooded physical abuse perpetrated by the High Inquisitor, Dolores Umbridge. Here too, a rationalization can be made: The fear of admitting that Voldemort was truly back led much of the wizarding world, including the Minister of Magic himself, into hysterical denial. Once again, however, a rationalization is far from a justification. When Umbridge cannot force Harry to recant his claim that the Dark Lord has returned, she sentences him to a week of detention, during which he is forced to write, hundreds of times, "I must not tell lies" with a pen that magically and excruciatingly etches into his flesh the words he writes on the paper.

The true-to-life terrifying corollary to this abuse is Harry's unwillingness to confide it to others. At first, he does not even tell Ron and Hermione, and he never agrees to tell McGonagall or Dumbledore. The reason he gives in his own mind is that he feels that the matter is something between him and Umbridge. Yet Harry's approach closely mirrors the tendency of victims of child or spousal abuse to remain silent, out of shame or some misguided notion that they "asked for it." It is to the discredit of Hogwarts, as a whole, and Dumbledore, in particular, that such an activity could go on unchecked. One has the feeling that Dumbledore should have known.

Therein lies a sensitive spot in all the *Harry Potter* novels. Somehow, an atmosphere has been allowed to flourish at Hogwarts in which students who are confronted with issues beyond their capacity to solve are afraid to approach adults for assistance. The assumption seems to be that the adults wouldn't understand or would blame the students for their predicament. Perhaps this might be understandable in the immature thought processes of a first-year student, but the feeling persists throughout the series. It often helps as a plot device when it is necessary to justify Harry's going off on his own to pursue his latest heroics, but one hopes that young readers do not absorb distrust for the adults around them and feel that they must handle everything on their own.

Finally, there is a form of professorial misconduct that is stressed much more in Jewish sources than in the *Harry Potter* saga. When a religious guide presents his ideas in such a fashion that they lead to misunderstanding and misapplication, he is held accountable. *Ethics of the Fathers* records that "An error in teaching amounts to an intentional sin."[23] In the realm of unacceptable beliefs, it warns: "Sages, be careful of your words, lest you be liable to a punishment of exile, and be exiled to a place of evil waters. When the students who follow you drink these waters, they will die, and the name of Heaven will thereby be profaned."[24]

J.K. Rowling tends to downplay the significance of unqualified teachers feeding students mistaken information by making most such teachers buffoons in the eyes of their students. The inaccuracies of Divination Professor Trelawney are depicted as either silly, if you see through them, or harmless, if you don't. The portrayal of Amycus and Alecto, Death Eaters stationed at

Hogwarts by Voldemort, as small-minded, uneducated, and evil makes it unlikely that the views they express in the classroom will be heeded. And so we come full circle to our original observation: Rather than just transmit information, teachers must be role models who mold the spiritual character of their students. Once teachers accept that responsibility and establish that relationship, their students will become receptive to the lessons the teachers yearn to teach.

We will let the Rabbis have the last word: "May the dignity of your students be as precious to you as your own."[25]

# SOCIETY

※

## PREJUDICE

## THE QUILL AND THE WAND

## OWNERSHIP

# Prejudice

J.K. Rowling uses the *Harry Potter* novels as a platform for combating racial prejudice. She succeeds because she does not lecture, but instead illustrates the effects of prejudice, and portrays it as the mind-set of the most unappealing of characters. And she is not afraid to take a playful jab at herself for being so earnest in her position.

By far, the most virulent racist in the series is Voldemort himself, who envisions a world in which those not of pure wizarding blood are relegated to second-class status and denied basic human and wizarding rights. This form of racism shares the most in common with the biological strain adopted by Adolf Hitler and Nazi Germany. There is nothing a "mudblood"—someone of only non-magical heritage—can do to be adopted into the ranks of the "purebloods," just as Hitler was committed to the destruction of the Jews, not their conversion. Voldemort's Death Eater followers absorb his thinking and his vocabulary. It was the very word *mudblood* that was the last straw in the relationship between Lily Potter and Severus Snape. When he used it, perhaps out of simple habit, she never forgave him. Lily understood that the racist mind makes its hideous actions acceptable by creating a new vocabulary to describe those it persecutes. Jews as human beings are harder to kill, but as Christkillers, vermin, or subhumans, they become an irritant that can be exterminated with impunity.

But the *Harry Potter* novels illustrate a key point when it comes to prejudice: It is not enough merely not to be a Death Eater. There are fine and upstanding citizens who would never condemn another on the basis of bloodline, and yet practice a quiet form of racism in their attitudes and behaviors. A member of the Order of the Phoenix, who would fight and even die to protect the rights of Muggles (non-magical folk),and those of mixed Muggle and magical heritage, would think nothing of accepting the subjugation of house elves and the stereotypes regarding goblins, not to mention ostracizing werewolves. Here the most delicate work must be done. By presenting a werewolf as Harry's most understanding teacher and half-giant Hagrid as the most likable gamekeeper, Rowling quietly makes clear that anyone who would judge such species as inferior is way off the mark. By having Harry save Griphook and benefit from his help, she softens our attitude toward goblins, while not negating all the negative stereotypes associated with them.

The most inspiring treatment of a persecuted species is reserved for house elves. True to form, Rowling presents us with Dobby, who develops through the books from comical to heroic, finally stealing the seventh movie with his proclamation: "I am a free elf and I have come to save Harry Potter." By the time Dobby meets his fate, readers and moviegoers alike feel for him and lament his fate. But then there is S.P.E.W. (the Society for the Promotion of Elfish Welfare), Hermione's organization for protecting elf rights. By choosing a comical acronym, and entrusting the endeavor to the ever-earnest Hermione, the author makes the point that, even when you are fighting for a righteous cause, you should take the cause seriously but not yourself. It also becomes clear that you cannot change society's assumptions all at once.

One group, however, seems beyond the requirements of civil treatment—the gnomes. For reasons never made clear, it is acceptable to brutally uproot them from their garden homes and even to stun one and turn it into a Christmas tree ornament. The only champion of gnome distinctiveness is—hold onto your hat—Xenophilius Lovegood, who tells his daughter Luna that if you are bitten by one you may hope for a gift of a new talent. We are as likely to adopt an enlightened attitude toward gnomes as we are to send our rabbi a gift subscription to the *Quibbler*.

As an oft-persecuted minority, Jews are particularly sensitive to the issue of prejudice, and we absolutely bristle at accusations that we are guilty of doing to others that which has been done to us. We are even more touchy about any claim that the Bible itself might sanction racial prejudice. A few observations may be helpful in this regard.

The Bible's repeated insistence on not oppressing the stranger, the widow, or the orphan cultivated a sense of compassion in the Jewish community for those whose status in society is precarious.

The Talmud stresses that accomplishment, not birth, should be the standard of judgment, as noted in this passage: "A scholar of illegitimate birth takes precedence over a high priest who is ignorant."[26]

No less a scholar than Maimonides maintains that the righteous of all nations have a share in the World to Come.

The modern State of Israel is a true melting pot of people of various skin colors, geographical origins, and languages. The

Ashkenazim, Sephardim, Yemenites, Ethiopians, Russian émigrés, Israeli-Arabs, and those of other groups have merged to form a society that, if not quiet or perfect, is at least functional.

All this is not to say that there are no sources in the Bible or Jewish literature that can be exploited to justify racism or that there are no individuals who have availed themselves of those sources. But such views have the necessary critical counterweights to lead to a just and welcoming society for all.

In the end, the battle against racism and prejudice—in life, as in literature—is a work in progress.

# THE QUILL AND THE WAND

The final confrontation between Voldemort and Harry pits Avada Kedavra against Expelliarmus. Both are spells of physical force, propelled by words. And the road leading to that moment, as well as the final minutes before the two opponents raise their wands, are filled with the clash of words—Harry's version of events versus Voldemort's distortions. Truth versus falsehood. Accuracy versus misrepresentation. Harry's battle involves the quill and the tongue as surely as the wand.

Throughout the series, Voldemort seeks not only to kill Harry, but to assassinate his character. And he isn't alone in this. Harry has almost grown immune to the ways in which Draco Malfoy and Professor Snape seize every opportunity to discredit him, when, during the Tri-Wizard Tournament of Book 4, he falls prey to Rita Skeeter. Eager to sell papers, Rita will stop at nothing to get her scoop. By eavesdropping as an unauthorized Animagus, inventing quotes with her Quick-Quotes Quill, and fabricating intrigue where none exists, Rita shows Harry for the first time the power of the quill, when wielded irresponsibly.

As infuriating as Skeeter's words are, they are mild compared to the campaign waged by Cornelius Fudge and the *Daily Prophet* in Book 5 to defame Harry in order to preserve the illusion that the Dark Lord has not truly returned. And even that barrage is tame, compared to what the *Daily Prophet* writes about him in Book 7, when its agenda is set by Voldemort himself.

Seen from this perspective, the novels read as cautionary tales of what can happen to a free press when it is corrupted by greed, politics, and, finally, dictatorship.

Harry and his friends do not accept these campaigns of words passively. Hermione discovers Rita's Animagus secret and uses it to silence the reporter. Harry fights the *Daily Prophet* assault in Book 5 by granting an interview to the *Quibbler,* in which he airs his side of things. And Lee Jordan and friends come to the rescue when Voldemort's propaganda machine is churning out hatred. By founding, in effect, Radio Free Hogwarts, they made sure that people could raise their spirits with a dose of the truth.

Different languages and cultures have adages that encapsulate the uneasy relationship between the power of the word and the power of physical force. In English we say, "The pen is mightier than the sword." A Midrash teaches that "The book [the Bible] and the sword descended from the heavens intertwined: If you observe what is written in the one, you will be delivered from the other."[27] These catchphrases emphasize that, ultimately, the word will prevail over the sword. Other sayings attribute to words the power normally associated with weapons: Life and death are in the "hands" of the tongue. It is not coincidental that the same Bible that is concerned with the conquest of the Land of Israel is equally concerned with the conquest of one's speech. From tale-bearing to slander to vulgarity, the list of verbal offenses chronicled in the Bible is long and detailed.

There are certain characters in Scripture who are forever associated with the sin of slander and character assassination. One is Doeg the Edomite, whose slander leads King Saul to execute all the priests in the city of Nov, after accusing the high priest, Achimelech, of conspiring with David against the throne.[28] The remarkable thing about Doeg's words is that they are absolutely true. He reports truthfully that David came to Nov and that Achimelech provided him with food and the sword of Goliath, and petitioned God on his behalf. It is what he neglects to mention that makes his words the trap that they are. He doesn't bother to add that Achimelech had no idea that David was fleeing Saul at the time (David intentionally withheld that fact). He does not mention that David had frequently passed through Nov on the king's missions, and received help from the priest. His grouping of three cherry-picked items in one compact sentence makes it sound as if the assistance rendered had been carefully planned out in advance between the two. No doubt, if challenged on his words, Doeg would have proclaimed, "But everything I said was true."

One of the regulations regarding illicit speech in Jewish law is that negative speech need not be explicit. Implying the negative notions or creating the negative result indirectly is also forbidden. Rita Skeeter would have done well to heed this. One of her favorite methods of slander is to present an incomplete set of facts—for example, the fact that Ariana Dumbledore, the sister of Albus, was not seen outdoors—and ask the reader to speculate on possible reasons, with special weight given to the most scandalous ones—could it be that Ariana's parents were imprisoning her? One can't blame her for conclusions drawn by her readers, can one?

Voldemort's preferred method in taunting Harry is likewise to ascribe to him the most selfish motives. Knowing full well how many times Harry has faced him alone, he still asks, "Who is going to fight for you this time, Potter?" Aside from the patent falsity of the claim, it is guaranteed to evoke guilt in the sensitive boy who blames himself for the deaths of his parents, Sirius, and Dumbledore. Voldemort is following the tried-and-true method of bullies and anti-Semites: Blame the victim to justify the crime. Pharaoh does it—*I have to act against the Hebrews before they overrun us.* Hitler did it—*The Jews are scheming to control the world.*

Words, even when unaccompanied by spells, can be lethal.

But they can also be therapeutic. A recent book exploring this dual power is titled *Words That Hurt, Words That Heal.*[29] And the healing power need not be a spell, either. Just think of the words with which Mrs. Weasley conveys to Harry that he is a member of the family. Or the words with which Harry makes clear to Ron during their first trip on the Hogwarts Express that he has much too much candy and it is only natural to share it. Or the words at the end of almost every volume, in which Dumbledore eases yet more of Harry's anxieties and answers more of his questions. There isn't a spell in the lot, but they do perform their particular magic.

Now think of some more words that could be heard in Muggle society—in its schools and synagogues, and other places of gathering: "You're new around here—let me show you around." "Could you join us for lunch?" "Sit at my table."

It's only appropriate to close with a few words from the headmaster himself: "Nitwit, blubber, oddment, tweak."

# OWNERSHIP

How do you own something? What makes it yours? And when do we say that it passes from your hands to someone else's possession?

Ask Voldemort or Dumbledore, Harry or Griphook, and you'll get very different answers. And Jewish law has something to say about each.

## Conquest

In Voldemort's way of looking at things, conquest is everything. "There is no good and evil—there is only power and those too weak to seek it." The murder of a witch or wizard is the means of possessing a "fabulous object"—a ring, a locket, a cup. Voldemort snatches the Elder Wand from the tomb of its former owner under the mistaken notion that such "conquest" will acquire it for him. It would have, but Harry had previously gained its allegiance by disarming Draco Malfoy. The fact that the Elder Wand has changed hands throughout history in exactly such a bloody fashion serves to underscore its questionable value. Dumbledore sought to retire the wand from circulation without yet another cycle of violence and conquest. His plan backfired, to Harry's advantage, and is reinstated by Harry, when he replaces the wand in the headmaster's tomb.

Jewish law recognizes ownership through conquest, but with misgivings and limitations. To begin with, the right to wage war is carefully limited within the Bible and Jewish law, and may not be exercised unilaterally by any ambitious monarch.[30] In the event of a justified war, property legally acquired during the war belongs to the victor. Nevertheless, just as one wizard can forcibly take the Elder Wand from another, in Jewish law, military conquest is seen as ultimately temporary, since force can undo force. The sanctity of the Land of Israel, conferred by the conquest of Joshua and the Israelites, is undone by the subsequent Babylonian conquest.[31] On the other hand, the re-sanctification of Israel, when Ezra and Nehemiah lead the return from the Babylonian exile, is viewed by Jewish law as permanent. One great Rabbi[32] explains the difference by saying that the second time the land was sanctified by the presence of God, and not the force of human arms. Such holiness is not reversible. "Not through valor, nor strength, but rather through my spirit, says the Lord of Hosts" (Zach. 4:6).

## Creation

In Book 7, Griphook the goblin expresses a fascinating theory of ownership: You own something by virtue of having made it. A goblin forever owns the silver piece he fashions. He may temporarily transfer that right through a sale, but, upon the death of the purchaser, the right of ownership reverts to the object's creator. Thus, both the sword of Gryffindor and the tiara of Auntie Muriel belong to the goblin who made them, or his heirs.

Jewish law has a similar, though less radical concept. According to some views, a craftsman who is given an item to repair obtains partial ownership of the item, to the extent of the value of the work, until he is paid for his labors.[33] The right of ownership, however, is limited in scope and duration. This model has been used to explain the biblical description of God as "acquirer (or owner) of heaven and earth" (Gen. 14:19). Since a craftsman gains a limited right of ownership by dint of his enhancement of an object, God, who created the entire world from nothing, thereby gains total right of ownership over it.

It is interesting that the Bible does view one transaction as intrinsically temporary in nature and incapable of permanence— namely, the sale of Land in Israel. According to the Book of Leviticus, one cannot permanently sell one's ancestral estate; all sales revert in the Jubilee year to their original owners. The reason is explicit: "And the land shall not be sold eternally, for all the land is mine, for you are but strangers and sojourners with me" (Lev. 25:23). No, God is not a goblin. In most business dealings, we apply the verse: "The heavens are God's, but the earth He has given to man" (Ps. 115:16), but in God's own chosen headquarters, the Land of Israel, the ownership He attains by virtue of creation remains absolute.

## Noble Intention

Albus Dumbledore understands that in order to accurately assess who deserves to possess an object, one must take motivation into account. The charm he places upon the Sorcerer's Stone in Book 1 prevents it from being possessed by anyone who wants it for personal use. Quirrell can see it in the Mirror of Erised, but only Harry, who doesn't want to keep it, can obtain it. By his own admission, Dumbledore falls short in his motivations for possessing the Deathly Hallows. Because he merely wants to tame it, and not to seek power with it, he is allowed to own the Elder Wand. But the invisibility cloak, which he takes in "vain curiosity," cannot work for him. And the Resurrection

Stone, which he dares to wear for selfish reasons, carries the curse that all but ends his life.

There is a similarity between this theory of ownership and a rabbinic philosophy of charity. The wealth that God grants us, this explanation goes, is not our personal property, but His, and we are mere stewards over it. Those who use their wealth for charitable endeavors will merit continuing in their financial position. Those who see the wealth as their own, will see it transferred to a more reliable steward.

## Owning through Disowning

Harry Potter succeeds where his teacher had failed and is able to unite the powerful Hallows precisely because he chooses to battle with Voldemort rather than indulge his own obsession with the Hallows, and because he is willing to abandon the wand and the stone for the greater good. In a sense, he comes to own the Hallows specifically through the act of disowning them. This altruistic trait is reminiscent of a particular type of Hasidic story, in which the righteous individual, or *tzaddik*, gains the World to Come by virtue of being willing to forgo it for a higher cause. In one such story, a couple comes to Rabbi Israel Baal Shem Tov,[34] pleading for a blessing to have a child. When the *tzaddik*, touched by their entreaties, swears that they will have their prayers answered, a voice from Heaven proclaims that these people were naturally barren, and since God will now be required to change nature to fulfill the oath of the Baal Shem Tov, the *tzaddik* will lose his share in the World to Come for forcing the issue. Upon hearing this, the Baal Shem Tov declares joyously, "I have always feared that my service of God was tainted by my hopes for reward in the hereafter. Finally, I can serve God purely, without ulterior motive of any kind." The heavenly voice then returns to say that, for his willingness to sacrifice his place in the World to Come to help this couple, the Baal Shem Tov will have his share restored.

What the Baal Shem Tov exemplified in eighteenth-century Russia had already been modeled by King David, in the period preceding his ascension to the throne. When young David and his men return from the site where the Philistines are massing to fight the Israelites, they find their adopted city in ashes despoiled by Amalekites, their wives and children taken captive, and their property plundered. David's erstwhile followers, blind with grief, turn on him. Bereft of his family, his possessions, and his leadership status, David has nothing left to call his own, except what comprises his essential core and identity. And deep inside himself, deeper than dwells "I have," he finds the "I am" of his soul. "David strengthened himself in the Lord his God" (I Sam. 30:6). The man who had everything, even when he had nothing, could be entrusted with the reins of the nation of Israel.

And perhaps that is the ultimate lesson: It is not individual ownership per se that is evil, as Communism argued in its day. But the passion of possession can possess one's soul and blind one to the more refined and elevated pursuits of life. One's grip of ownership must be a loose one. One must be willing to possess nothing in order to be worthy of possessing everything.

# WHAT REALLY MATTERS

⚡

## CHOICE

## PROPHECY

## DEATH

## GOOD AND EVIL

## LOVE

# Choice

On his first evening in Hogwarts, as first-year students are being sorted into one of the four houses—Gryffindor, Slytherin, Hufflepuff, and Ravenclaw—Harry Potter has his first identity crisis. The Sorting Hat, which has rapidly assigned other eleven-year-olds to their respective houses, hesitates when placed on his head. "You would do well in Slytherin," it insinuates into his ear. Remembering that Slytherin is known for producing dark wizards, Harry begs, "Anything but Slytherin," and finds himself assigned to Gryffindor. From that moment, Harry is plagued by doubts regarding his essential nature. Why did the hat almost assign him to Slytherin? As the years pass, his doubts only increase. Why do he and Lord Voldemort have so much in common? Why is he a parselmouth, able to speak the language of serpents, a trait almost exclusively associated with the dark wizards of Slytherin? Who is he deep down? These doubts are only intensified by his friends, who instinctively recoil when they hear him speak to a snake.

Finally, he voices his fears to Dumbledore at the end of Book 2, and the headmaster wisely replies, "It is our choices . . . that show what we truly are, far more than our abilities." Harry may have all the natural abilities of a dark wizard, but he still has the freedom to choose the path of his life. Over and over again, Dumbledore teaches Harry that, notwithstanding nature, nurture, or even prophecy, we are the architects of our own destinies.

No character in fact or fiction illustrates this idea better than King David. Young David is first introduced to the reader as *admoni*—red-haired or ruddy-complexioned, a term used to describe only one other biblical character: the bloodthirsty Esau. The Talmud explains the predisposition of some people to bloodshed in an astrological vein, saying that anyone born when Mars, the red planet, is dominant ("Mars is bright tonight," says Firenze the centaur in Book 1) will spill blood.[35] But that predilection, says the Talmud, can be fulfilled by a person through a commendable deed, a neutral deed, or through the crime of murder. The implication is clear: David has the potential to become an Esau, spilling blood over every perceived slight.

That potential remains dormant for years, as young David rises in the service of King Saul. The only blood he spills is that of Goliath and other enemies of Israel. Far from becoming an Esau, he is depicted with imagery and language associated with Jacob. He works for his father-in-law, as Jacob did. He is promised one daughter, then given the other. He pays double the bride's price agreed upon. His father-in-law seeks to kill him. There are several Hebrew terms that appear almost exclusively in the Jacob and David stories.[36] The Bible seems intent on having the reader identify David as a Jacob-like character.

But all that changes abruptly. When refused food by his distant relative, Naval the wealthy Carmelite, who heaps on abuse for good measure, David instructs his men to gird their swords and rides off to murder Naval and his entire household. Suddenly, David is described as the leader of a band of four hundred men, the exact number commanded by the biblical Esau. Avigayil, the wise and beautiful wife of Naval, intercepts David and attempts to dissuade him from following through on his violent intentions. She brings him a gift of food and calls it a *beracha,* the exact term Jacob uses for the gift of animals he sends to Esau. The reader is meant to understand that David is facing a crisis of identity. Will he continue to be the righteous Jacob figure, fighting only the battles of the Lord, destined to be the founder of a dynasty of monarchs in Israel? Or will he surrender to the Esau potential in his soul and kill to feed his bloodlust and avenge his personal insult, thereby disqualifying himself from the throne? With the help of Avigayil, David succeeds in making the right choice.

Harry and David both teach that we are not the helpless victims of our genes, our predispositions, or a toxic upbringing. While nature and nurture exert an influence on our lives, we have the freedom of choice to transcend their influence and dictate the course of our lives. And with that ability comes the responsibility to do so.

# PROPHECY

In a world where lies abound and truth is hard to come by, the word of God has always been held up by believers as the ultimate trustworthy source. Catchphrases like "It's God's own truth" or "the gospel truth" bear out this idea, as do the practices of swearing by God's name or while holding a Bible. So when God sees fit to directly communicate with human beings through the gift of prophecy, it would stand to reason that the prophetic message should be taken as embodying absolute and unassailable truth. It may, then, surprise us to discover that while the worlds of the Bible and *Harry Potter* may differ on who is worthy of prophecy and what is its source, they agree that prophecy is most definitely *not* the last word.

Let me explain.

In Judaism, the qualifications of a prophet are very steep. The highest moral behavior must combine with intense preparation and even then, prophecy is only a possibility. Because of these requirements, the sages struggle to explain why someone of the character of Balaam the sorcerer could receive communication from God.

Prophecy in the wizarding world, on the other hand, bears no connection to the moral stature of the person who delivers the message. Sibyll Trelawney, the divination professor, is a faker and a drunk. She has elevated faking to such a level that she herself does not believe that she is faking. And yet it is she who twice delivers prophecies concerning Harry and Lord Voldemort. She predicts the birth of the child who will be the Dark Lord's nemesis, and later foretells when Wormtail will reunite with his master at the end of Book 3. She is the vehicle for these prophecies, but she is unaware when she is uttering them. They just *happen* to her.

This concept of prophecy is not a religious one. Perhaps because J. K. Rowling so carefully avoids religion in the series, we do not get a sense of the source from which prophecy emanates. Rather that being a communication from a Higher Being, prophecy seems to be a power of nature, accessible only to those coincidentally born with the necessary receptivity. It is like being an idiot savant or having a photographic memory—a quirk of wizarding biology. The closest parallel in Jewish sources is the Talmudic statement that when prophecy was taken from the prophets, it was granted, instead, to the deranged.[37]

Whether prophecy is a communication from God to the righteous or a rare additional brain function, both worlds refuse to allow its word to be the last word. In Book 6, despite Voldemort's obsessive attempts to obtain the prophecy about the child who would challenge him, Dumbledore takes great pains to explain to Harry that accepting the validity of the prophecy is a choice, not a given. "You see, the prophecy does not mean you have to do anything! But the prophecy caused Lord Voldemort to mark you as his equal . . . In other words, you are free to choose your way, quite free to turn your back on the prophecy."

Voldemort accepts the prophecy, and acts on it. By assuming that Harry is the boy whose birth was foretold, and not Neville Longbottom, who meets the same criteria, and then by trying to kill baby Harry, rather than waiting until he becomes a threat, Voldemort gives Harry some of his own abilities and creates the very threat that he is trying to eradicate. Harry, on the other hand, recognizes that his struggle against Voldemort is undertaken willingly, and not simply because of the words of the prophecy. Had Voldemort not guided his actions based on the prophecy, it need not have come true in quite the same way.

Biblical commentators use the same principle to answer a philosophical question that arises in several stories. Here is how the dilemma is phrased in two of the cases: Since God tells Abraham that his children will be slaves in a strange land, why is Pharaoh punished for simply fulfilling the prophecy?[38] Likewise, once the prophet Nathan tells King David that, as punishment for having taken Bathsheba, the wife of Uriah, his own wives will be publicly taken by another, why is Absalom considered guilty for having taken his father's wives? One answer given in such cases is that a prophecy of this nature does not compel a particular person to act on it. If we choose to ignore the prophecy, it can find its fulfillment under different circumstances.

Which, of course brings us to a related subject that also applies to both worlds—the discipline of astrology. Here, too, wizards and Bible scholars can find common ground in maintaining that even if the stars are to be believed, their message is so malleable as to allow for multiple modes of fulfillment. The centaurs, portrayed as masters of heavenly signs, are objects of both admiration and frustration. They inspire admiration in that, unlike the haphazard predictions of Trelawney, their predictions are grounded in long observation and actual knowledge. But they frustrate us because their knowledge of the complexities and multiple possibilities makes them speak in vague generalities ("Mars is bright tonight") and almost never act on their theories. It is only during the Battle for Hogwarts, for instance, when the battle of good versus evil is so blatant, that the centaurs finally take a side.

Many Midrashim develop the idea that astrological predictions, even if granted credence, can be fulfilled in multiple ways. This flexibility is seen as part of God's plan, allowing Him to adjust matters according to the needs of the moment. One famous example concerns the ultimate fate of Moses. According to the Midrash, Pharaoh's astrologers recommend drowning Hebrew babies in the Nile because they foresee that the deliverer of the Jews will meet his downfall because of water. What they do not foresee is that the water in question is the water Moses is asked to coax from a stone in the wilderness. By hitting the stone, rather than speaking to it, he brings down God's wrath.[39]

Another Midrashic strand traces God's reinterpretation of an astrological reality to benefit the Israelites. When Moses demands the release of the Israelites from Egypt, Pharaoh responds, "Behold, for Ra is upon you!" (Ex. 10:10). The word *Ra* is a double entendre that can mean "evil" in Hebrew or can refer to the Egyptian sun god, Ra. Taking the second possibility, the Midrash reads into the verse a warning that Pharaoh is issuing: If the Israelites leave at this astrological moment, they will be destroyed by the Egyptian god, who symbolizes blood. Following this thread through later verses, the Midrash reinterprets Moses's plea to God after the sin of the golden calf. "Why let the Egyptians say, 'He took them out when Ra was ascendant'?" (Ex. 32:12). God's response to Moses's prayer is reinterpreted by the Midrash to mean, "God changed the meaning of Ra." According to the Midrash, God changes the meaning of "Ra" from the blood of destruction to the blood of circumcision, which the Israelites perform upon entering the Land of Israel.[40] This string of Midrashic comments assumes that there is validity to the astrological claim made by Pharaoh, but that God uses the inherent flexibility of all such forecasts to influence events to the advantage of the Hebrews. In an explanation that echoes the religious nature of prophecy, the Talmud declares, "The constellations do not influence the fate of the Jewish people."[41] Just as righteous behavior can make a person worthy of prophecy, so does such behavior lead God to recast astrological forecasts to benefit the righteous. Through leading the right kind of life, we can be assured that our fates are not left to the impersonal stars or any arbitrary system.

# DEATH

*To the well-organized mind, death is but the next great
adventure.*

> —Albus Dumbledore (Book 1)

Lord Voldemort is so terrified of death that he rips his soul into
seven parts to avoid it.

Albus Dumbledore, on the other hand, says that there are
things in this world worse than death. Judaism would agree.

What could be worse than death?

Certainly, the kiss of a dementor, which leaves its victim
soulless and mindless, would be worse than death. But Dumbledore means more. He means that there are ways of living to
which death is preferable. A life lived in betrayal of one's principles is a living death. Peter Pettigrew, who betrays James and
Lily Potter to Lord Voldemort to save his own neck, should rather have died, as Sirius Black told him in Book 3. His cowardly
life from that day on is merely a parody of living. He is just
marking time until his own evil catches up with him. The same
fate could have awaited Severus Snape for his role in the betrayal, but he redeems himself with years of service, protecting
Harry and informing on the Death Eaters.

The Talmud teaches that there are three cardinal sins that
one must avoid, even on pain of death: murder, idolatry, and

certain forbidden sexual relationships. At a time of religious persecution, one must lay down one's life rather than violate even a minor custom. In the Bible, Daniel is prepared to die in the lions' den rather than bow down to a statue of the king. Hananiah, Mishael, and Azariah face the prospect of death in a fiery furnace rather than cease praying to God (Daniel 3). The underlying concept is that life without faithfulness to God's will is meaningless.

What is it about death that so unnerves Lord Voldemort that he is willing to murder numerous times and explore the darkest magic to achieve immortality?

It may well be that Voldemort's fear of death is based on a belief that death is final, with nothing to follow. Dumbledore, on the other hand, believes that death is part of the cycle of life, a stage in a drama that goes on and on. When Harry asks Dumbledore in "King's Cross Station," at the end of Book 7, where he will go if he chooses to board a train rather than return to life, Dumbledore answers, "On." Judaism believes in an afterlife of the soul, known as the World to Come, as well as a resurrection of the body. The exact nature and chronology of these times, as well as how they interweave with the messianic era, is debated by Jewish philosophers, but Jewish thought is clear that this world is not the final destination of the soul. In fact, the *Mishna* even calls our world a vestibule, or corridor, leading into the palace that is the World to Come.[42] Hasidim tell of an encounter between a Hasidic rabbi and a czarist interrogator. The interrogator brandishes a revolver and demands information, bragging that "This little toy has induced many prisoners to talk." The rabbi responds calmly, "That little toy works well on people with many gods and only one world, but I have only one God and two worlds."[43]

Voldemort sees death as an enemy—either he eats you or you eat him. Hence the term *Death Eaters*. He sees submission to death as shameful, picturing Dumbledore in the "ignominy of death." Like the brothers in Beadle's tale of the Hallows, Voldemort seeks to conquer death, unwilling to admit the impossibility of the task. For Dumbledore, death is to be faced, if not welcomed, and after death there is rebirth. No wonder he founds the Order of the Phoenix in the belief that life can emerge from the ashes of death, just as a new phoenix is born from the ashes of the old. Dumbledore wisely understands that death cannot be defeated, nor should it be. But its looming presence can lend urgency and preciousness to the tasks of life. Every lesson Dumbledore gives Harry in Book 6 is lent greater significance by the spreading of the curse that will eventually take his life.

In a verse of Psalms and a terse Midrash, Judaism encapsulates the gifts of death. The verse is this: "Teach us to number our days, that we may form a wise heart" (Ps. 90:12). The realization of our limited time on earth is supposed to inspire a wise use of that time. And the Midrash on the verse in Genesis 1:31, where the narrative sums up creation ("The Lord saw all that He had done, and behold it was very good") comments: *very good* refers to death.[44]

But ceding the ultimate victory to Death does not mean relinquishing every battle along the way. While for Voldemort, the struggle seems to be an all-or-nothing proposition, the Bible and the headmaster of Hogwarts see the value in how one meets death and choreographs the scene of one's death. When God tells Moses that the time has come for Aaron to die, Moses accompanies his brother up the mountain. There, the Midrash fills in, they find a cave with a bed and a single candle burning. Under Moses's direction, Aaron removes his priestly vestments and his son, Elazar, dresses himself in them for the first time. Then Aaron ascends the bed, gently folds his limbs, and closes his eyes, and the Lord takes his soul gently. Moses is so impressed with the choreography of Aaron's death that he petitions God for the same type of death when his time comes.[45]

Albus Dumbledore retains control over the manner and timing of his death. Instead of yielding to the curse Voldemort put on the Resurrection Stone, he chooses to die when it best advances his plan. Instead of dying at the hands of Voldemort, Bellatrix, or Draco Malfoy, Dumbledore contrives to have Severus Snape do the deed. And he, like Aaron, leaves the world knowing that his "son," Harry, will continue his life's work.

The true vanquishers of death are those who sense death's inevitability but continue to live heroic lives, accomplishing their life's mission for as long as they are able, maintaining their dignity and civility in the face of deteriorating physical conditions, and never allowing death to rob them of the *tzelem elokim,* the image of God reflected in every human being. Stories abound of individual Jews during the Holocaust who went bravely to meet the beast, with *tefillin* on their head or the *Shema* on their lips. Like Harry in the graveyard at the end of Book 4, they resolved to meet death standing erect, face-to-face, fully knowing they did not have the resources to stave off the end.

But this type of heroism is not limited to concentration camps. In my years in the rabbinate, I have seen it more than once. I've seen it the patience of a man stricken with cancer whose deteriorating condition left him less and less in command of his limbs. I've seen it in the faith and gratitude of the mother of one of my congregants, who, throughout her terminal illness, would inspire others and profusely thank every health-care professional or visitor who entered her hospital room. And I've seen it in the indefatigable efforts of patients who try treatment after experimental treatment, in hopes of gaining a few more days to spend with their dear ones. Most recently, I saw it in the courage of a parent in the school where I teach. This hero was diagnosed with a severe form of leukemia, and the disease proved resistant to two bone marrow treatments. When the doctors could no longer recommend a treatment to win his battle, he decided to spend his remaining time as productively as possible, and, in a letter to family and friends, invited them to commit themselves to avoiding negative speech for the duration of his life. As of this writing, both his challenge and his life are holding out.

# GOOD AND EVIL

At its most basic, the showdown between Harry Potter and Lord Voldemort is a restatement of the eternal struggle between good and evil. Every epic attempts to express truths about that clash, which is at the center of the message of the Bible, as well. "Behold I have placed before you today life and good and death and evil" (Deut. 30:15). No examination of these two works can be complete without discussing at least a few of the aspects of this mammoth subject through the dual lenses that have informed all of our explorations.

The eternal nature of the struggle is a point not lost on the wizarding world. As he tells Harry more than once, Dumbledore always expects that Voldemort will return. It is only a matter of time. Much of the first four books is spent attempting to delay that return. As Dumbledore says at the end of Book 1, "It is important to fight, and fight again, and keep fighting, for only then can evil be kept at bay, though never quite eradicated."

In this struggle, one can often identify three camps by their reactions to evil. There are those who collaborate, those who combat, and those who are silent. In the *Harry Potter* novels, the dementors and Fenrir Greyback, the werewolf employed by Voldemort, are examples of collaborators who join forces with Voldemort and the Death Eaters with an eye toward gaining more prey for themselves. Members of the Order of the Phoenix are committed to combating the menace. Cornelius Fudge, the minister of magic, who denies the return of the Dark Lord until it is impossible to ignore, exemplifies those who are silent, thereby allowing the evil to spread. Until Dumbledore forces him to choose, Professor Slughorn hopes to walk the tightrope of neutrality in the battle, as do the centaurs, until the final battle.

These groupings are discernible in biblical and historical settings, as well. The Midrash paints a picture of Pharaoh consulting three advisors about his plan to enslave the Jews. Balaam eggs him on. Jethro flees. Job is silent. Each receives his just desserts: Balaam is ultimately killed. Jethro is rewarded and becomes Moses's father-in-law. Job is afflicted with all the trials described in the Book of Job to see if the pain will induce him to break his silence.[46]

The same camps reassert themselves in the attitudes of those who come in contact with David as he flees from King Saul. The king's own son, Jonathan, and daughter, Michal, actively support David against the unjust designs of their father. The Ziphites and Doeg the Edomite, on the other hand, conspires to hand David over to be executed. And the people of Ke'ila, whom David saves from the Philistines, while grateful, would have allowed Saul to extradite David, had he made the demand.

Survivors of the Holocaust relate sadly how some non-Jews were more eager than their Nazi allies to contribute to the extermination of the Jews. The Final Solution could not have been implemented without what Daniel Goldhagen has termed "Hitler's willing executioners."[47] By contrast, there were the Raoul Wallenbergs and Oskar Schindlers, the Chiune Sugiharas and other righteous gentiles who risked their lives to save Jews from the ultimate evil. Many, however, fell into the category of the silent, to the point that Pastor Martin Niemoeller wrote his famous poem decrying silence:

In Germany they first came for the Communists,
and I didn't speak up because I wasn't a Communist.

Then they came for the Jews,
and I didn't speak up because I wasn't a Jew.

Then they came for the trade unionists,
and I didn't speak up because I wasn't a trade unionist.

Then they came for the Catholics,
and I didn't speak up because I was a Protestant.

Then they came for me —
and by that time no one was left to speak up.[48]

The tools used for combating evil appear to place the forces of good at a disadvantage. In his debate with Voldemort in Book 7, Harry asserts that Dumbledore was just as capable as Voldemort of delving into the black arts, but, because of the kind of person he was, refused to do so. Harry himself is unwilling or unable to fight with the curses that come so naturally to his enemies. When he first tries the Cruciatus Curse on Bellatrix Lestrange, after she kills Sirius, she laughs at him and tells him, "You have to mean it!" Apparently, even when he thinks he is full of hate, Harry has too much love to wish such harm on others. Whenever Harry crosses spells with Voldemort or his henchmen, from the dramatic close of Book 6 to the final duel in Book 7, his spell of choice is the disarming spell, Expelliarmus, not the killing spell, Avada Kadavra, favored by the Dark Lord. He is so loath to use anything else that the Death Eaters are able to figure out who the real Potter is at the beginning of Book 7, despite numerous Polyjuice impersonators, based on his choice of spell.

To some degree, Jewish thought also shuns using the tools of the wicked, even on the wicked themselves. The Talmud tells how a great sage, at his wits' end from the persecutions of his neighbors, resolves to pray that his enemies die. His wife, however, corrects him, asking him to pray that they repent, rather than be punished.[49] We so regret the need for punishment that we symbolically pour drops of wine, like tears, as we tell at the Passover Seder of the vengeance wreaked upon the Egyptians.

In a very modern context, Western armies face the same dilemma in fighting terrorism. What do you do when terrorists fire at you from buildings housing civilians, and place children on the rooftops to prevent you from bombing them? One reporter, when interviewing an expert in battlefield ethics, asked "whether we are capable of continuing to defend ourselves, practically and morally, against enemies that often have no moral compunctions. Are we capable, that is, of surviving, protecting ourselves, without sinking to their level?"[50]

Embedded in the imagery of the disarming spell versus the killing spell is the idea that the righteous do not destroy the wicked, but rather the evildoer's own wickedness recoils upon him. It is not Harry's spell that kills Voldemort, that is, but Voldemort's own killing curse that rebounds, just as it did when Harry was only a baby. It would seem that just as a skillful batter has the knack for using the speed of a pitch to propel it powerfully in the opposite direction, love has the power to deflect the violence of evil and focus it upon its originator. Voldemort found this out the hard way when he aimed the killing curse at baby Harry. In Book 7, he is retaught that lesson with finality.

The Bible clearly endorses the notion of the wicked self-destructing, at least in some cases. The Psalmist says, "He dug a pit and fell into the ditch he himself had made" (Ps. 7:16). But there can be times when the righteous have no choice but to actively combat evil with whatever tools are available. When Moses sees an Egyptian taskmaster beating a Hebrew slave, he instinctively strikes and kills the oppressor. When an entire city turns idolatrous, the Bible calls for all its inhabitants to be put to the sword, its property burned, and its land left desolate.[51] This is a far cry from Expelliarmus.

While this may be a more realistic view, which admits that sometimes you can't fight evil without getting your hands dirty, it must then answer the question of what becomes of those who use the devil's tools to fight the devil. Will those who killed Osama Bin Laden be forever desensitized to the value of life; for, after all, they have killed, albeit in the service of justice? Do Jewish sources have something to say about this question?

It happens that they do. Biblical commentators have suggested an answer based on an extra word in the biblical text. After exhorting the Hebrews to utterly destroy everyone and everything in the hypothetical idolatrous city, the Bible promises reward to those who comply: "The Lord will give you mercy, will have mercy upon you and multiply you" (Deut. 13:18). Noting the repeated reference to *mercy,* an eighteenth-century commentator explains that the first instance is a Divine promise that those forced to be ruthless and take life in the service of the law will be blessed that their actions will not desensitize them nor leave them callous to the infinite value of human life. They will be given back the mercy they thought they had lost.[52]

Just as those of good will hesitate to employ the methods that evildoers use without compunction, so too, are those with good intentions prone to introspection and self-doubt—states of mind that never seem to trouble the forces of evil. What's more, evildoers are always willing to fan the feelings of inadequacy among their adversaries by accusing those of good will of exactly what they fear most. Before their final duel in Book 7, Voldemort taunts Harry by claiming that he had always allowed others to fight and die for him. As false as this claim is—and, fortunately, Harry is able to refute it—Voldemort knows that it will hit Harry where it hurts most, jabbing at his sense of responsibility for the deaths of Sirius, Dumbledore, and probably even his parents. Yet Harry does not fall into Voldemort's trap by succumbing to paralyzing guilt.

When Korach rebels against Moses in the wilderness, he accuses the Hebrew leader of seeking to amass power. Moses's response, before saying a word, is to fall prostrate on the ground. A Hasidic master interprets Moses's gesture as introspective: Before responding with a denial and counterclaim, Moses wants to make sure that the claim is not true in some deep recess of his heart. Only after ascertaining that does he dare to speak a word in his own defense.[53]

The forces of good are often outnumbered. Members of the Order of the Phoenix comprise a relative handful who have to stem the growing tide of Death Eaters, not to mention those under the Imperious Curse. In the Bible, Jonathan, the son of Saul says it best: "The Lord has no impediment to saving, whether through the many or the few" (I Sam. 14:6).

And often it boils down not merely to the few, but to the one. History can hinge on the actions of one individual, whether his name is Harry or Moses or David. These individuals bear immense responsibility, and are subjected to severe tests. Great sacrifices are demanded of them, and (in the words of acclaimed science fiction writer Lois McMaster Bujold) they are tempted to "give away their heart to gain their heart's desire."[54]

Dumbledore himself admits to not telling Harry about the prophecy that his struggle with Voldemort is a struggle to the death because of the immense burden doing so would place on Harry. Harry comes to believe, and even tells Slughorn, that he is "the chosen one," with all the responsibility that entails. It is hard to imagine any scenario for the defeat of Voldemort if Harry shirks his mission.

The biblical view is not as emphatic regarding the indispensability of one individual. While Moses plays a pivotal role in leading the Israelites out of Egypt, ultimately, it is God who gets the credit, and, on the night of the Passover Seder, the name of Moses does not even appear in the *Hagaddah*. Although Queen Esther receives credit for saving the Jewish people, when she hesitates, she is told by Mordechai, "If you are silent at this time, salvation shall come to the Jews from another quarter, but you and your father's house shall be lost " (Esther 4:14). The rabbinic adage captures this idea: The Lord has many messengers. If God wants something to happen, it will happen. Those who assist will receive eternal credit, but God's plan will prevail— with them or without them.

The chosen individual is tested sorely. Each of the *Harry Potter* books ends with a major confrontation, and almost all contain the phrase *He was alone.* Harry is led to a moment when all he can call upon is his courage and the lessons he has learned. With those tools and his wits he must battle basilisk and dementor, treacherous teacher and Death Eater, and, of course, Voldemort himself.

The concept of *nisayon,* or "test," in the Bible is strikingly similar. When "The Lord tested Abraham" (Gen. 22:1), and commanded him to sacrifice Isaac, there are to be no witnesses, no cheering crowds, no film crews—just an old man and his long-awaited, supremely cherished son both ascending Mount Moriah, with only one to descend. Of course, future generations will witness the heroism through the medium of the Bible, but that is unknown to the two principals at the time.

More trying even than the physical tests are the psychological roadblocks. Harry's hurdles center around the loss of his mentors—being deprived of his parents, Sirius, and Dumbledore—the abuse he suffers at the hands of Snape and Umbridge, and the campaigns to discredit him. Abraham's test, as understood by the Midrash, had a major psychological component. The Midrash populates the solitary three-day journey to Mount Moriah with visits from Satan in various guises. At one point, Satan appears as an old man who is astonished at what Abraham intends to do. When he cannot dissuade Abraham, he makes this chilling prediction: Tomorrow, God will call you a murderer for listening to him today. The great Bible teacher Nechama Leibowitz observes that all of Satan's arguments are really arguments going on in Abraham's mind, trying to square God's command with all that he knows about God and the morality that God teaches.[55]

How can he throw away all the years of preaching of a kind and benevolent God?

And just as Abraham has to be willing to sacrifice what is nearest and dearest, so do all crusaders for good. Ron has to be willing to allow himself to be knocked senseless in the wizard chess game at the end of Book 1. Hermione has to cast a memory charm that will cause her parents to forget her, in order to ensure their safety. It is in the area of sacrifice that J. K. Rowling may herself have sacrificed realism for a happy ending. In the classic formulation, the champion who vanquishes evil and saves the world cannot find a place for himself in that redeemed world. Moses does not make it to the Promised Land. Frodo the hobbit saves Middle Earth, but does not find rest within it and must sail off into the mist. Realism demands that Harry be victorious, but scarred; instead, Book 7 concludes that his scar had not pained him for nineteen years, and "All was well."

Finally, the champions of good are offered opportunities to achieve their heart's desire, but in order to do so, they must pay with their very heart, betraying their core principles. Harry is propositioned by Voldemort at the end of Book 1: If he joins Voldemort, he will be spared. Otherwise, he will meet the "same end" as his parents, and they will have died in vain. In the movie version of the scene, Voldemort actually offers to bring Harry's parents back, if Harry joins forces with the Dark Lord. Harry's two-word answer—"You liar!"—makes clear where he stands.

It could be argued that Moses is offered a similar temptation. After the Children of Israel construct and worship their golden calf, God tells Moses, "Leave me alone and I shall destroy them, and make a greater and more powerful nation from you!" (Ex. 32:10). Moses refuses to take the bait, responding, "If you forgive them, [well and good], but if not, erase me from the book you have written" (Ex. 32:32). Had Moses agreed to the destruction of the Israelites, he would not have been worthy of siring a new nation. His greatness lies in his unswerving dedication to the nation he has brought out of Egypt. God, unlike Voldemort, gives him enough of a hint to make the right choice. As the Talmud notes, the words *Leave me alone* are superfluous—was Moses holding God's sleeve and preventing Him from acting? In fact, God is hinting that the choice is Moses's. He can defend the Hebrews, and single-handedly prevent God from destroying them. God as much as invites him to play defense attorney. Moses does, and the rest is history.

Can evil ever be totally defeated? From Dumbledore's words to Harry in Book 1, we would think not: "While you may have only delayed his return to power, it will merely take someone else who is prepared to fight what seems a losing battle next time—and if he is delayed again and again, why, he may never return to power." Yet Harry does vanquish Voldemort in the climactic duel of Book 7. We are left to wonder in the epilogue whether, nineteen or ninety years later, evil will again rear its head, and demand once more the heroism and sacrifices of another Harry.

The biblical vision of the end of days, when the House of God will be well established on the mountaintop, when the lion and the lamb make peace and saviors ascend Mount Zion to finally judge Mount Se'ir, offers the promise of a time of ultimate redemption, when "Death shall be swallowed forever, and the Lord God shall wipe the tears from every face" (Isaiah 25:8).

# LOVE

*The one with the power to vanquish the Dark Lord approaches . . . but he will have power the Dark Lord knows not.* (Sybill Trelawney, Book 5)

It takes seven books and thousands of pages for Harry Potter to appreciate the words of the prophecy. And Voldemort never does.

Time and again, Dumbledore tells Harry that the secret to his survival and to his ultimate superiority over Voldemort lies in the power of love:

> If there is one thing Voldemort cannot understand, it is love. . . . to have been loved so deeply, even though the person who loved us is gone, will give us some protection forever. It is in your very skin. (Book 1)

> You would be protected by an ancient magic of which he knows, which he despises, and which he has always, therefore, underestimated—to his cost. I am speaking, of course, of the fact that your mother died to save you. (Book 5)

Voldemort cannot understand that the secret of Harry's survival has been his mother's sacrifice. He attributes Harry's resiliency first to accident, then to the twin cores of their wands, and finally to his need for the Elder Wand—but never concedes that it could have been love. Even when Harry, following his mother's example, sacrifices himself in the forest to protect all those in Hogwarts, Voldemort cannot understand why his silencing charm could not bind them. Throughout the saga, Voldemort inspires fear, not love, in his followers, because he has no love to spare them, only cold, calculating use to make of them. Even when Bellatrix Lestrange betrays a kind of love or adoration toward him, Voldemort is incapable of responding in kind, and shuns her touch. Because he cannot fathom the love of a mother for her child, he cannot imagine that Narcissa Malfoy will betray him, announcing that Harry is dead, in order to get into the castle of Hogwarts to search for her son, Draco. And because he cannot understand the love of Snape for Lily Potter, it never occurs to him that, in killing her, he has turned Snape into a spy for Dumbledore.

Harry, on the other hand, effortlessly gives and receives love. He faces danger in each book in order to protect others. His impulse, in the Tri-Wizard Tournament, is to save Fleur's sister, Gabrielle, even at the risk of forfeiting his task; this is an expression of his deepest nature. There is no logic to the gesture. Had he thought it out, he would have realized that Dumbledore and the tournament officials would never have allowed an innocent hostage to come to harm. But the thing about Harry is this—when it comes to love and sacrifice, he functions on an instinctive, not a premeditated, level.

The centrality of love finds an answering echo in biblical and Jewish sources. From the verse "The world is built on kindness" (Ps. 89:3), to the Mishna that lists loving-kindness as one of the three pillars of the world,[56] to the scriptural example of love conquering self-interest in the relationship of David to Jonathan, the son of Saul,[57] there is no doubt as to the place that love occupies in the system of biblical values. And yet, in many sources love shares the spotlight with fear, combining to form a balanced spiritual personality. *Ethics of the Fathers* urges us to "Be like servants who serve the master with no thought of reward"[58]; that is, to serve God out of love. Yet *Ethics* concludes, "But may the fear of heaven be upon you." Love is the primary motivator, but must be supplemented with awe. The medieval commentator Nachmanides reinforces this hierarchy by explaining that when positive and negative commandments conflict, the positive ones take priority over the negative, because performing positive commandments is motivated by love, while refraining from prohibitions stems from fear.

Both Harry and Voldemort inspire loyalty in others. But the loyalty of Voldemort's followers is self-serving, what the Mishna in Avot calls "a love dependent upon something." Harry doesn't focus his admirers on himself, but rather on an ideal for which he is prepared to sacrifice. Voldemort uses his followers for his own power-hungry ends; Harry educates his followers to give as he does.

Voldemort's ignorance of love backfires in yet another way: All his attempts to neutralize Harry are violent. Had he understood the love through which Dumbledore inspires Harry and through which Harry, in turn, inspires others, he would have attempted to win Harry's allegiance, rather than trying to destroy him. Voldemort would have been a much more dangerous foe had he wielded the power of love as a weapon.

Voldemort's inability to love might have been rationalized as the result of a childhood without parents and their unconditional love. But then there is Harry—also deprived of parental love, raised by callous relatives, and yet so receptive to love.

Does Harry choose to love or is the trait innate, "in his skin," as Dumbledore characterizes his mother's protection? Is it only instinctive, as suggested above, or is there a volitional aspect as well? One need look no further than his rescue of Malfoy from the Room of Requirement at the end of Book 7 to see the choice involved. Six books make it abundantly clear that there is little lovable about Draco. As Harry's rival, his attacks have been growing in violence and effectiveness. When he ambushes Harry in the desperate moments of the search for the diadem of Ravenclaw, he forfeits any right to consideration. Most likely, Harry's choice is aided by his recollection of how Dumbledore had tried to save Malfoy from himself at the very moment that Malfoy was trying to kill him up in the astronomy tower at the end of Book 6. But the message is that, beyond any innate tendency to love, love can be learned by example and chosen by those who have every right to hate.

I know this to be true. I write these last lines through closing eyelids at an overnight retreat for a group of eighty fifth-grade students. Last night, at 2:30 a.m., a student interrupted the light sleep I had finally entered after settling the kids down for the night: "Rabbi, my stomach hurts a lot and I feel like I'm going to throw up." My day had begun at 5:30 the previous morning, officiating at services in a house of mourning for a member of my synagogue whose father I had buried the day before. There were other adults who might have comforted the boy who called my name, but they were fast asleep. Tending to nauseous eleven-year-olds was not in my original programming when I rolled off the assembly line. But since then I have experienced my mother staying up with me, when I sat gasping steam congestedly as a child. I have become a father and seen my wife spend countless nights tending to our children, from nightmare to nebulizer. And I have had the good fortune to teach in a school where going the extra mile for a student is the norm, not the exception. I sat up with the boy. I helped him throw up and clean up. I lent him my iPad—the same one on which I type these words—so that he could get through the night watching movies. Toward morning, I realized that I hadn't even asked him his name.

The point is—the point of it all is—that people can learn to love. If only they choose to.

# KIDS WRITE ABOUT HARRY POTTER

S ince 2001, I have been running *Harry Potter* evenings in my school, and encouraging kids to write on subjects related to *Harry Potter* and ethics. They have written on subjects ranging from "Lessons of Life I Have Learned from Harry Potter" to "Harry Potter and Judaism" to "Bullying in the World of Harry Potter." And one fine year, as the kids were growing impatient waiting for Book 5 to appear, I formed the Harry Potter Club for the express purpose of showing the students that they could write the fifth book—or their version of it—themselves, while they waited for J.K. Rowling to finish hers. This chapter is devoted to showing how Harry Potter has not only gotten kids to read; it has gotten them to write as well. My thanks to the young writers and their parents for their kind permission to reproduce their words here.

# LESSONS OF LIFE

**Galit Wernick, Grade 7**
**Friendship**

In *Harry Potter,* there are many lessons we can learn, but one special one is about friends and friendship. One of the most important lessons about friendship is also one of the hardest: All friends fight. Even best friends fight and make up. So in Harry Potter, Hermione starts off with a bad relationship, but then becomes best friends with Ron and Harry.

To be friends with someone you must also sacrifice to help them. In the first book, Ron sacrifices himself for Harry and Hermione in a game of chess. Hermione is also always helping the boys to solve their mysteries. In the second book, Ron is terrified of spiders but he still goes into the forbidden forest and follows the spiders, risking his life. Harry fights the basilisk with no weapon, even though he knows the basilisk is deadly.

Friends must also know that there can't be just one person who gives everything and one person who does nothing but stays in the group. You have to be like Harry, Ron and Hermione.

Treat your friends with respect, honor and trust. Harry, Ron and Hermione never interrupt each other. They always treat each other with respect. They also trust each other with their lives and most of their secrets. There is also no person who is left out or talked about behind his back.

Friends should never expect anything outside of kindness, loyalty, respect, honor or trust. You don't need to do anything to get in the group, like doing something dangerous, embarrassing or stupid. You also must not expect them to always be doing the work—you must do some work too, or it's not a fair friendship. You know you are expecting too much when you are doing no work to keep the friendship going, but, at the same time, are hurting their feelings and calling them names. This is certainly not the case with Harry, Hermione and Ron . . .

**Tamar Herman, Grade 6**

In the book series *Harry Potter,* Harry, Ron Weasley and Hermione Granger have a very tight friendship. Whenever one of them needs help with something, they go to the others. The first time I read the books, I noticed nothing peculiar about the relationship. Then I read them again, and noticed how, once Harry and Ron became friends with Hermione, the whole story was more touching. In the first book, you saw how Ron got captured in chess, and how Harry made Hermione turn back and hopefully save all three of them.

Sometimes, when someone picks on one of my friends, I remember how Draco Malfoy picked on Harry and his friends. When I remember this, I just try to help my friend. When I do this, it's like I'm saying a spell to make the bully back away. I wish the books had more of an impact on people to be good because the books helped me decide that. I also wish the books could help more people to be a better friend, as they helped me.

## Shara Feit, Grade 6

We can learn a few lessons of bravery and friendship from Harry Potter. Harry Potter can teach us something, just as Moses did. At first, Moses is on his own, running away from Egypt so that he can be spared. Harry, instead of running away, confronts his fears as a first-year student, and succeeds in beating Voldemort, at least for now. Moses also confronts his fears and God protects him, but his fears aren't confronted until he feels that he has enough strength to do so. Harry just goes in and does the best he can and succeeds. Even though what Harry did was a little "braver," what Moses did was a little more sensible.

We hear the voice of sensibility from someone else: Hermione. She decides that because her two parents are muggles, she has to become the smartest and the most sensible. Hermione does this when Ron and Harry, both from wizarding families, do average, and sometimes awful work. She lends a hand to her friends by helping them study, and, in the first book, her knowledge saves the lives of all three of them from the Devil's Snare. At first she is cautious and doesn't want to help out of fear of being expelled and degraded even more. Even though she is scared, she helps out and realizes the meaning of true bravery: doing something you think is impossible and will never ever happen. In conclusion, we learn from Hermione that you have to help your friends when they really need you, even if there will be serious consequences. However, you should only do things with major consequences if your friends really need you.

We can learn almost the same thing from Harry Potter's other friends. When Harry, imprisoned in his own house, isn't able to go to Hogwarts, the Weasleys come along and rescue him and his owl, Hedwig. From there we see an instance of "Love thy neighbor as thyself." That situation also had consequences, in the reaction of Molly Weasley.

Dobby the house elf teaches us something entirely different. He has good intentions (to save Harry), but instead gets Harry into even more trouble than he was in already. He goes too far to protect him. Would you like your mail to be intercepted and to live in prison in a home that was already torture? I know I wouldn't. How about getting locked away from a school that is so fun that it's like summer vacation? NO again. We learn from Dobby that even if you care a lot about somebody, you should let them be their own person and make their own personal decisions. All of these lessons are about bravery and helping out, but not helping too much. Everybody should be brave when it's needed but don't jump off a cliff when somebody says, "On your mark, get set, *go!*" These are four life lessons that we learn from Harry Potter and the characters in his books.

# THE VALUE OF PEOPLE'S LIVES IS THE SAME

### Maayan Rosenfield, Grade 5

A lesson that I think J.K. Rowling meant to teach us in *Harry Potter* is that the value of each person's life is the same even if people are different. A way you can learn that is that all of the villains were mean to all of the half-bloods but J.K. Rowling does not let the villains get away with it.

The Book of Leviticus (19:30) says that you should treat strangers who might be different the way you treat someone who is the same as you, because you were once different in Egypt.

In Egypt, the Israelites were treated badly just because they were the Israelites. The midwives and Egyptians were told to take away people's lives just because the King had this crazy, made-up idea that the Israelites would take over the land and make the Egyptians leave. The King is afraid of them because they are different. This verse teaches us that you should not be afraid of differences and that the value of the lives of different people is the same.

Voldemort tries to kill Hermione because she is a "mud-blood"—from nonmagical stock. I think that maybe the reason he did this is that he was scared of the difference between them.

In Book 1 of *Harry Potter,* when Hermione is stuck in the girls' bathroom with the terrible troll, even though she's not Harry and Ron's favorite person because she is smart and she's a little bit of a show-off at the beginning, they still know she's a person. They go and save her, even though it means putting their lives in danger.

From Harry and Ron's behavior and from the Torah, we and Voldemort should learn that the value of each person's life, no matter who they are, is the same. Hashem created everyone equal.

### Talia Lavin, Grade 7

A lot of courage is shown in the books. Harry stands up to the scariest guy in wizard history more times than you can count and boy does he stand up for his friends!

But Harry isn't the only one that we can learn from. Remember Neville? Dumbledore says, "It's harder to stand up to your friends . . ." If your friends, or, more likely, the popular people you've been trying to get close to, are doing drugs or robbing, if you don't stand up to them, it's like you're helping them.

Let's get back to Harry for a second. Harry is the guy we all wish we are: His special powers are discovered by people other than those who raised him. He's suddenly famous, *and* he can blast people with his wand! But wait a second—he has the most dangerous wizard of all time after him, plus a really nasty archrival. So maybe Harry's life isn't so perfect after all, teaching us not to take it for granted that someone else's life is better than our own.

What about Hermione? She certainly works hard—maybe too hard? Remember the time-turner? That pretty little fiasco teaches us not to bite off more than we can chew.

Ron is kind of poor. He has a big family and a small house. How would you feel if you came from a background like that and your best friend was famous and rich? From this guy we learn loyalty—he's a good friend to Harry even if they fight a few times.

**Ayelet Senderowicz, Grade 5**

I've learned many lessons from *Harry Potter,* but I think the main one is really that magic can't solve everything. Even if you are the most accomplished witch or wizard ever, there will still be some times when magic just won't be the answer. For example, in a friendship situation, such as a fight, you can force your friend to do what you want using the Imperious Curse, but they won't be acting of their own free will and you will know that. Also, if someone sees too much and you put a Memory Charm on them, do you honestly want to erase their entire memory or just the part that they saw? Magic is limited; it can't help

KIDS WRITE ABOUT HARRY POTTER

you with issues such as love and/or death. Harry himself was in that situation (his parents' death). I think that I might have to rephrase the lesson as follows: It might seem that magic has solved your problem, but you'll always know that you did something wrong by using magic and that God will know in Heaven and judge you there.

Another lesson is that sometimes you need other people (friends) to help you with things. Harry was in that situation when he wanted to go track down the horcruxes by himself, but Ron and Hermione insisted on going with him. It turned out that without them, Harry might not have tracked them all down and destroyed them. Another example is that if you're doing a worksheet and can't figure out a problem, you might ask your friend for help. Then you wouldn't be doing it all by yourself. This lesson is similar to the first lesson, because they both involve your choices and actions, so be careful what choices you make.

**Sahar Segal, Grade 7**

*Harry Potter* is not a series of books just to read for fun. Everyone can learn lessons from the books. One of these lessons is that even if you're fighting for the right cause, it doesn't mean that you are perfect and do everything good and right. Another one is that alone you can't do anything, but if you work together, you can achieve almost any goal.

One lesson from *Harry Potter* is that even if you're fighting for the right cause, you don't do everything right or good. We learn this from every book in the series. Even though Harry, Ron and Hermione fight for the good of the world, they break many rules and do many things wrong. For instance, they make Polyjuice potion, breaking many rules and gaining absolutely

★ 95 ★

nothing. This helps us in life because from this we learn that nobody is perfect. No matter what they do or how amazing they are, they are not perfect. If someone gives the impression that they are perfect, something is wrong. We learn this from the second book, from the character of Guilderoy Lockheart. Everyone thinks he is perfect—he's a powerful wizard, handsome, brave, great, etc. But in the end, he is discovered as a fraud, and the only spell he can perform is the Memory-Erasing Spell.

Even Harry isn't perfect, and the author makes sure we don't think he is. He is resourceful, brave, and kind, and possesses a knack of surviving every ordeal. But he is a troublemaker and not the smartest person in town. We must remember this over the course of our life . . .

The last lesson is that alone you can't do many things, but together we can achieve almost anything. Harry, Ron and Hermione wouldn't have gotten anywhere if they were working alone. In the second book, Hermione discovers what the monster is and what it does. She basically discovers the answer to the mystery. Harry kills the basilisk, defeats Voldemort and saves Ginny. Ron saves Harry and Hermione from many uncomfortable situations, and is willing to risk very much to save his friends. He is the one who frees Harry from the Dursleys. He also realizes when the Polyjuice potion effect is wearing off, he shows Harry the full spider situation, and he is always willing to help his friends. It is easy to break one stick, but almost impossible to break many sticks put together. This is a very good and useful thing to remember.

**Ariel Shay, Grade 6**

In all of the *Harry Potter* books, Harry Potter never hurts anyone for fun. Draco Malfoy is the opposite of Harry. Draco loves to tease, hurt, or do anything mean to anyone.

An example of this is the story of Neville Longbottom's rememberall. Draco took it and flew up on his broomstick to put the rememberall on the roof where Neville couldn't get it. Harry defends Neville by following Draco up into the air to get the rememberall back and return it to Neville. Doing this, Harry is breaking a rule by not listening to what Madame Hooch said about not flying while she took Neville to get his wrist fixed. In this case that is OK because Harry is doing it only so that he can get back the rememberall, and that is a good deed. When Draco throws the rememberall, Harry takes another risk by following the rememberall, even though he barely knows how to fly.

Every time we do a good deed, God rewards us. In Harry's case, Professor McGonagall rewards Harry by making him the Gryffindor seeker.

When a troll gets into Hogwarts, Harry thinks of Hermione first. He and Ron run to save her from the troll, without thinking about themselves first. This is another mitzvah. Ron only hurt the troll because he was saving Hermione. Harry even jumped on the troll, which was a really big risk. Harry and Ron were awarded five points each in thanks for their "rescue." Hermione was aware that the boys had had a chance of getting themselves to safety or saving her. She knew that if she didn't speak up, they would get punished instead of rewarded. Hermione even lied to get the boys what they really deserved.

In the fourth book, during the last challenge, Harry could have easily beaten everyone, but each time he heard a cry, he ran in that direction. He kept helping everyone else out instead of just winning.

# HARRY POTTER AND THE BIBLE

### Rikki Feuerstein, Grade 6

*Laban* (in Hebrew) means white. White is a pure color. The black in Sirius Black's name is a dark color that stands for evil. But why would Laban have a name that implies good, and Sirius have one that implies evil? Perhaps it is a question of appearances. Laban looks like a very nice guy. After all, he ran out to hug and kiss Jacob at the well. Sirius is described as a bad-looking person. But both of these impressions are based on outward appearances and are false. The inner self of Laban and Sirius was the exact opposite of their appearance.

### Yonatan Sturm, Grade 5
### The Burning Bush versus the Burning Wardrobe

In *Harry Potter and the Half-Blood Prince,* Dumbledore and Harry travel to Voldemort's orphanage through the pensieve. They use Dumbledore's memory in order to get there. When they arrive at the orphanage, they watch Dumbledore invite Voldemort to Hogwarts. Voldemort had known that he had some special powers, but he did not know what those powers meant or how to control them. Those powers scared him because he was alone and he had no one to help him. When Dumbledore asked him to come to Hogwarts, Voldemort seemed excited and scared. He was happy that Dumbledore understood that he was a wizard and nervous that he was going to go someplace new that had rules and requirements. Voldemort asked Dumbledore to prove that he was a wizard and Dumbledore made Voldemort's wardrobe burst into flames. The flames died out and the wardrobe was not burnt! Now Voldemort believed what Dumbledore was telling him.

This reminds me of Moses and the burning bush. Moses is living in a foreign country without his father and mother, and he does not realize the special strengths that he has. One day, God speaks to Moses from a burning bush, and tells Moses that he will lead the children of Israel out of Egypt. At first Moses is scared of what God is telling him. He does not feel confident that he can be this great leader. Then he recalls that even though the bush is burning, the branches do not get burnt. This is a sign to Moses that God is the ultimate leader who will help him lead His nation to freedom.

Just like Moses, Voldemort realized that he was powerful when he saw something burn and not get burnt. However, Voldemort used his power for evil. He became feared by everyone and wanted to destroy anything that was in his way. Moses used his power for good. He led his nation to freedom and wanted to teach everyone the good ways of the Torah. Moses was loved and not feared. I learned from this that Torah is truth and guides people to do mitzvot and good things.

# GRATITUDE

**Anonymous, Grade 7**

I feel that we can learn a lot from *Harry Potter* that applies to us, even as Jews. We learn bravery and perseverance. Most of all, though, especially from a Jewish point of view, we learn the trait of gratitude.

The Hebrew term for gratitude is *hakarat ha-tov*, or recognizing the good, because it means looking past the evil someone has done to remember the good things he once did. In the third book, Harry is told that it was really Peter Pettigrew who sold Harry's parents to Lord Voldemort. But as Sirius Black and Professor Lupin are about to cast the fatal spell, Harry stops them. He explains that James Potter would not have let Sirius and Lupin go through with it. But I think the reason goes a little deeper. Neither James nor Harry can kill Peter Pettigrew because of gratitude. At one point in time Peter was friends with James, and at that time Peter was a good person. That's why they couldn't have killed him even after he betrayed the Potters.

Another instance of gratitude takes place during a Quidditch match in the first book. During the game, Professor Quirrell tries to knock Harry off his broom with a spell, but Professor Snape was protecting Harry but chanting a counterspell. Snape was trying to save Harry out of gratitude for the one good thing James Potter had done for him in saving his life.

To connect this to the Bible, we can cite a story from Chapter 2 of the First Book of Kings. King Solomon decides not to execute Eviatar the priest even though Eviatar had been part of a rebellion against him. Solomon spares Eviatar because of all the good things Eviatar had done for his father, David.

# LET MY PEOPLE GO! [Ex. 5:1]

## Noam White, Grade 6

Harry Potter had troubles basically the same as the troubles in the Bible. Here are five examples:

—In the beginning of the first book, Harry had to leave his aunt and uncle's house. The same thing happened to Abraham, who was commanded, "Go forth from your land and your birthplace, and the house of your ancestors to the land that I shall show you" (Gen. 12:1). Abraham was not very close with his father, as Harry was not close to the Dursleys, but it was still hard for them to leave home.

—When Harry's aunt and uncle would not let him go to Hogwarts, it was like when Pharaoh would not let the Israelites leave Egypt. The more the letters came, the meaner and more aggravated Harry's aunt and uncle became.

—Eventually, when Hagrid came, the Dursleys had to give in. The same thing happened when God brought upon the Egyptians the plague of the killing of the first-born—Pharaoh got scared and let them go.

—Another parallel is how Voldemort is always trying to kill Harry, but never succeeds. In the Bible, a lot of people try to destroy the Jewish people but never succeed.

—When Harry was holding the Sorcerer's Stone, he could not get killed. This is like the fact that if we stay with God, we will not be destroyed.

This shows that Harry Potter has a lot more in common with the Bible than the average person would suspect. This brings an old saying into play: "Never judge a book by its cover."

### Talia Lavin, Grade 7

Voldemort can be compared to King Saul, in that he was once handsome and strong and became much worse. However, he is different in the fact that he, unlike Saul, went searching for evil power and became twisted and malevolent. His presence in the books is like the Evil Inclination, evil and consciously so, but masking its evil to its victims. To Quirrell he says, "There is no such thing as good and evil—only power and those too weak to take it." This is definitely a mask over his evil. Quirrell, stuttering and weak as he was, wouldn't have been as easy to catch if Voldemort hadn't persuaded him, using words.

Voldemort is portrayed as fierce and bloodthirsty, but very strict about his servants' loyalty, as is shown in the graveyard scene at the end of Book 4. He may be dark and evil, but he has a seductive luster of power that is attractive to his followers.

Harry can be compared to Moses. He grew up with muggles, just as Moses grew up with Egyptians. Harry's childhood was not described in detail; neither is Moses's. He was a loner, like Moses, a solitary figure fighting for good. However, Harry is more physically vested in his battle with evil, while Moses's battle is primarily spiritual.

Dumbledore is a mysterious figure, enigmatically representing a father figure to Harry. He weaves in and out of the books, cryptically revealing information over the course of the volumes. In Jewish culture the only Dumbledorian figure is the big guy Himself—G.O.D. Dumbledore is "terrible in anger" and he's notably "the only one Voldemort's afraid of." Light's (Dumbledore's) struggles against dark (Voldemort) is the fundamental core of the book.

Dumbledore's speech to Harry: "You've delayed him, Harry. If others keep delaying him forever and ever, he'll never come back. . . ." And if we Jews keep fighting back in our stubborn, foolish, wonderfully stiff-necked, crabby way, we will continue forever and ever.

# GOOD, EVIL, AND THE BIBLE

### Adina Goldman, Grade 7

Harry Potter has very defined ideas of what is good and what is evil. Harry is good and Voldemort is evil. Good and evil are opposites. In the Bible, however, these separate concepts seem to overlap. A good person makes a mistake, while a bad person does a good deed. There are figures that cannot be characterized in either direction. Some of their deeds are righteous and well directed, while others are terrible, making these people difficult to understand.

Moses was an amazing personality and an extremely prominent figure in the Bible. One of the aspects of his character was his famed caring and compassion for others. Even though he was righteous, he wasn't perfect. After sinning, Moses wasn't allowed to enter the Land of Israel. He is an example of a good person who made some mistakes.

Esau, Jacob's twin, is an example of a not-as-common variety of person in the Bible. He was not a naturally good person. However, he still seemed to be able to do a little kindness. Esau was Isaac's favored child. The Bible says that Esau was a hunter, and he probably brought his father food. This is plainly an act of honoring one's father.

In the Bible, there are also figures with good intentions, whose deeds didn't reach the heights of the deed-doer's expectations. Reuben, son of Jacob, felt it was his duty as the eldest son to rescue his brother Joseph from the pit into which he had been thrown. He didn't succeed, however, because, by the time he arrived at the pit, Joseph had already been sold into slavery.

As well as people with good intent, there were people with bad intentions, whose deeds were transformed into better than they had intended. Balaam is an example of this kind of person. He was sent by Balak, King of the Midianites, to curse the Israelites. Instead, God made him bless them.

*Harry Potter* is related to Judaism in this: One's beliefs and actions greatly affect whether or not he or she is good. People do many things, not all "good" or all "evil." We trust God to weigh our good actions, thoughts, and beliefs against our bad ones to find if we are good or evil. God trusts us to try to be good people, and moreover, to try to make the right choices in life.

# Harry Potter and Ethics of the Fathers

**Sarah Meira Rosenberg, Grade 7**

(Editor's Note: *Ethics of the Fathers,* also known as *Pirkei Avot,* is a book of the Mishna devoted to ethical behavior and character development.)

In this essay, I wish to discuss ten particular statements from *Ethics of the Fathers* and their connections with the *Harry Potter* books.

1. In chapter one, Mishna 4, it is written:

*If I am not for myself, who shall be for me?*

This concept is demonstrated in Book 3. Near the end of the book, Harry must overcome dementors. There is no one to help him. He must help himself. He does, albeit in an unorthodox fashion. He really winds up *helping himself,* which is what this Mishna says.

2. *Who is wise—he who sees what is to come.* (2:13)

This clearly applies to Dumbledore. He knows immediately what to do in nearly every situation. Nothing seems to rattle him. He always seems to *know what's coming.*

3. *Who is mighty? He who conquers his evil inclination.* (4:1)

This, too, applies to Dumbledore. In Book 2, Harry tells Riddle that Dumbledore is the greatest wizard in the world, not Voldemort. According to this Mishna, Harry is absolutely correct, because Voldemort used his power for evil, and Dumbledore *overcame any evil inclination* he may have had and used his power for good—therefore Dumbledore is greater.

4. *Anyone who forgets even one thing from his lessons is like one who is obligated by the Torah to pay with his life.* (3:6)

This concept can easily be applied to Hermione, who treats every homework assignment, class, and exam as though it were a life-or-death situation.

5. *Judge every man favorably.* (1:6)

This can also apply to Hermione. After Harry's name came out of the goblet of fire, she believed that he had not entered the Tri-wizard Tournament. J.K. Rowling also shows the painful flip side: Ron not believing Harry about not entering, and having their friendship almost destroyed.

6. During the time that Ron and Harry were angry at each other, Hermione acted in accord with (1:12) as a "pursuer of peace." She tried to get them to make amends, and eventually succeeded.

Harry also acted as a pursuer of peace. He did so when Ron was convinced that Hermione's cat had eaten his pet rat, Scabbers. During that time, Harry tried to get them to be friends again.

7. These struggles to maintain their friendship make us wonder if Harry, Ron, and Hermione's friendship is a *friendship dependent upon something,* or a *friendship not dependent upon something,* to use the terminology of 5:20.

I think that it is "not dependent upon anything." Sure, they had disagreements, but the things that angered them were unpredictable. It wasn't as though Ron only agreed to be Hermione's friend if her cat wouldn't eat his rat.

8. Now let's move on to a different character, Draco Malfoy. We are warned to

*Distance yourself from a bad neighbor* (1:7). In the first book, Malfoy says exactly what the Mishna says, "You don't want to go making friends with the wrong sort." But then he adds, "I can help you there." He tried to take Harry away from his friends. That is definitely the mark of a "bad neighbor."

9. Another couple in *Harry Potter* has a famous trait mentioned in *Pirkei Avot*. Mr. and Mrs. Weasley must have taken a lesson from 4:1: *Who is rich? One who is happy with what he has.* They have the "We'll manage" attitude. They never complain about having "so many mouths to feed."

10. Characters are not the only things in *Harry Potter* novels that have characteristics mentioned in *Ethics of the Fathers*. Hogwarts itself possesses a characteristic mentioned in 1:5—

*Let your house be open.* Hogwarts lets poor people in, like Ron, muggle-borns like Hermione, almost squibs, such as Neville Longbottom, and just about anyone else.

I'd like to conclude with this thought: Just as Harry has the same characteristics that Salazar Slytherin prized in his students, so too do the characters and places in *Harry Potter* have characteristics prized by our righteous ancestors.

# WRITING BOOK 5

### Talia Lavin, Grade 6

Severus Snape was not happy. Now, he was never happy, but his face was unusually twisted, pinched and malignant. Snape's life was a gloomy one, but he had always wanted one thing—the job of Defense Against the Dark Arts teacher. And now, to have *his* job taken away by a mere Scottish good-for-nothing? For Professor Burtelle was not very impressive-looking. Her brittle greenish hair—dyed accidentally in a painful accident with essence of snozzdoodle—was thin, and her gigantic yellow horn-rimmed glasses scarcely improved her appearance. The decipher ability of her squeaky, rolling voice was much the worse for her Scottish burr. It was uncommon to see her without her pet owl, Scylla. Scylla had markings remarkably similar to her owner's horn-rims, and rumor had it that she was some nastily spelled relative.

But Professor Burkelle was not as silly as she appeared; her workbooks were in strict order—but one might note the way her Poisons ledger was ten times the length of the others. Whatever the reason, Snape was a bit wary—as well as weary—of the new teacher, for he was a cautious man.

# GLOSSARY

*Note:* Some of the following entries have been adapted from *Prayer Dictionary,* by Edith and Oscar Tarcov (KTAV, 1965).

**Esther (the Scroll of Esther):** The biblical book that tells the story of Purim, the holiday celebrating how a Jewish woman named Esther saved the Jewish community of Persia from extermination around the fifth century BCE.

***Ethics of the Fathers***: See *Pirkei Avot.*

**Haggadah:** The text of the service read at the Seder on Passover; it contains prayers, songs, and rabbinic texts about the Exodus and the obligation to retell its story.

***Judenrat* (Jewish council):** An administrative council that the Nazis required Jews to form within the ghettos during the reign of the Third Reich. These bodies served as liaisons between the Jews and the German authorities, administered all internal ghetto services, and were forced to provide lists of names to the Nazis for people to be assigned to slave labor and for those subject to deportation to the concentration camps.

***Lulav*:** A palm branch that is traditionally joined with willow and myrtle branches, which are then waved together alongside an etrog (citron) during the holiday of Sukkot.

**Menorah:** Can refer to the candelabrum found in the ancient Jewish Temple or the lamp traditionally lit during the eight nights of the holiday of Hanukkah.

**Midrash:** A form of commentary on a biblical passage, much like a sermon. There are two types, compiled into many volumes: Midrash Halakha (legal) and Midrash Aggadah (narrative/moral). Both use biblical verses as the basis for their ruminations.

**Mishna:** The Mishna is a Hebrew legal code, compiled by Rabbi Judah the Prince around 200 CE, based on a passed-down oral tradition. It forms the basis for the Talmud, which is structured as a commentary to its words.

**Mitzvah:** The Hebrew word for "commandment." The Torah is traditionally said to consist of 613 mitzvot, or obligatory commandments (248 positive and 365 negative). The word is often used colloquially to mean "a good deed."

***Pirkei Avot (Ethics of the Fathers)*:** A tractate of the Mishna that consists of collected ethical maxims of the rabbinic sages.

**Shabbat:** The Jewish Sabbath, or day of rest, which takes place each Saturday (beginning Friday at sundown).

***Shema:*** Central prayer of the morning and evening prayer services, drawn from the Bible. Its name derives from its opening words: *Shema Yisrael Hashem Elokeinu Hashem Echad*—Hear O Israel, the Lord is our God, the Lord is One. This monotheistic credo is also traditionally recited when an individual faces imminent death.

**Shofar:** A ram's horn that is ceremonially blown throughout the holiday of Rosh Hashana, the Jewish New Year.

**Simcha:** The Hebrew word for "joy" which can also be used to denote a happy occasion.

**Talmud:** An expansive postbiblical compendium of Jewish legal disputes, teachings, and stories, based around the Mishna and the books of the Bible and compiled from 300 to 500 CE. There are two Talmuds, each named after their place of origin: The more renowned and largely Aramaic Babylonian Talmud, and the Hebrew Jerusalem Talmud.

**Tefillin (Phylacteries):** Two small leather boxes which that contain four handwritten sections of the Torah and to which leather straps are attached and used to bind the tefillin to an individual's arm and head during prayer, in fulfillment of the biblical injunction, "You shall bind them [the commandments] as a sign upon your hand, and they shall be a reminder between your eyes" (Deuteronomy 6:4–8).

**Torah:** The biblical Five Books of Moses, or Pentateuch, which serve as the foundation for the Jewish faith and tradition. In broader usage, the term can refer to the entirety of the traditional Jewish canon, encompassing the Mishna, the Talmud, and the Midrash.

*Tzaddik:* The Hebrew word for "righteous" or "righteous one"; it is used to connote a righteous individual.

**Zohar:** The foundational work of Jewish mysticism (or "Kabbalah"), it is traditionally attributed to the Mishnaic sage Rabbi Shimon bar Yochai.

# ENDNOTES

*Note: BT = Babylonian Talmud*

## I. The Individual
### Breaking the Rules
1. This treatment is based on an analysis by Rabbi Hershel Schachter, *B'Ikvei Ha-Tzon* (Flatbush Beit Midrash, 2001).

### Manners
2. BT Avodah Zara 18a.
3. R. Tamir Granot, in a series of lectures on the Holocaust located at http://etzion.org.il/vbm/search_results.php?subject=שואה+ואמונה&koteret=שואה+ואמונה

### Repentance
4. BT Moed Katan 16b.

### Grief
5. Sixth-grader Yehudit Shuter.
6. Commentaries to Gen. 39:11.
7. Commentaries to Gen. 37:2.
8. *The Examined Life* (Touchstone, 1990), p. 29.
9. Hizkuni to Gen. 47:28.
10. *The Examined Life*, p. 30.

## II. Relationships
### *Friendship*
11. Deut. 34:8.
12. Num. 20:29.
13. BT Sanhedrin 6b.
14. Ibid. and *Ethics of the Fathers* 1:12.

### *Parents and Children*
15. Gen. 30:1.
16. Gen. 37:35.
17. I Sam. 2:19.
18. BT Taanit 4a.
19. Rabbi Yehuda Shaviv building upon an idea of Rabbi Abraham Isaac Kook (at http://www.vbm-torah.org/vtc/0025824.html).

### *Teachers and Students*
20. BT Bava Metzia 33a.
21. Rabbi Amnon Bazak about Rabbi Yehuda Amital at http://www.haretzion.org/component/content/article/14/76-hesped-abazak.
22. Recounted about the Rebbe of Bluzhov by Yaffa Eliach in *Hasidic Tales of the Holocaust* (Oxford University Press, 1982), pp. 13–15.
23. *Ethics of the Fathers* 4:13.
24. Ibid., 1:11.
25. Ibid., 4:12.

### III. Society
*Prejudice*
26. Mishna Horayot 3:8.

### The Quill and the Wand
27. Yalkut Shimoni Ekev 860.
28. See I Sam. Cp. 21–22.
29. Rabbi Joseph Telushkin, *Words that Hurt, Words that Heal* (Harper Paperbacks, 1998).

### Ownership
30. See, for example, BT Berakhot 3b.
31. See Maimonides, Mishne Torah, Terumot 1:5.
32. Rabbi Joseph B. Solovetchik, building on comments of his rabbinic ancestors. See, for example, Rabbi Hershel Schachter, *Nefesh HaRav*, 1994, p. 77.
33. BT Kiddushin 48b.
34. Rabbi Israel Baal Shem Tov (1698–1760): Mystical Rabbi and founder of the Hasidic movement.

### IV. What Really Matters
*Choice*
35. BT Shabbat 156a.
36. For example: *terafim, mira'ashotov, lama rimitani/rimitini.* For thorough treatment of the parallels between the stories, see R. Amnon Bazak, *Makbilot Nifgashot* (Tevunot Press, 2006). Much of this material can be found in the series of classes available at http://etzion.org.il/vbm/search_results.php?subject=שמואל+תנך &koteret=שמואל+בספר+שיעורים (Hebrew) and http://www.vbm-torah.org/shmuel.htm (English).

### Prophecy

37. BT Bava Batra 12a.

38. See Maimonides, Mishne Torah, 6:5; Nachmanides to Gen. 15:14.

39. See commentary of Rashi to Ex. 1:22.

40. See commentary of Rashi to Ex. 10:10.

41. BT Shabbat 156a.

### Death

42. *Ethics of the Fathers* 4:16.

43. Lubavitch Hasidim tell this story of Rabbi Joseph I. Schneersohn (1880–1950), sixth *rebbe* of Lubavitch.

44. Bereishit Rabba Parasha 9.

45. See Rashi to Num. 20:26.

### Good and Evil

46. BT Sanhedrin 106a.

47. Daniel Jonah Goldhagen, *Hitler's Willing Executioners* (Random House, 1996).

48. Martin Niemoeller (1892-1984).

49. Rabbi Meir and Beruria in BT Berakhot 10a.

50. David Horovitz interviewing Prof. Asa Kasher in the *Jerusalem Post,* April 22, 2011.

51. Deut. Cp. 13.

52. Rabbi Haym ibn Atar, *Ohr HaHaym Ha-Kadosh* to Deut. 13:18.

53. Heard orally attributed to Rabbi Menachem Mendel of Kotzk (1787-1859).

54. Lois McMaster Bujold, *Memory* (Baen Books, 2001). Bujold is a multiple Hugo award–winning science fiction writer.

55. Quoted in Nechama Leibowitz, *Studies in the Book of Genesis* (World Zionist Organization, Dept. for Torah Education, 1972).

**Love**
56. *Ethics of the Fathers* 1:2.
57. Ibid., 5:16.
58. Ibid., 1:3.